U.S. Trademark Law for Busy Entrepreneurs

Protect Your Brands Without the Hassle

Markavo.com

Contents

Foreward

There is a tenacious obstinance that beats in the hearts of many American entrepreneurs - that they should be their own lawyer. This book was born in the broken dream landscape of the trademark application junkyard. Over the years we have spoken with tens of thousands of *do-it-yourselfers* seeking help with their failed trademark applications. Some were initially led astray by the siren song of cheap "do it yourself" $35 form filing companies found on Google that offer no legal advice and almost guaranteed bad results. Others underestimated the mercilessness of their clever foe, the U.S. Trademark Examining Attorney. Examiners spend their day weaponizing thousands of pages of statutes and case law against the unprepared, self-represented trademark applicant. Trademark Examiners, after all, demonstrate that they are actually doing their job by issuing trademark refusals.

The goal of this book is to help you avoid self-inflicted injury by providing you with the preparation you need as a busy entrepreneur. This book will not show you step by step in exhaustive detail how to file your own trademark application. Why? The vast majority of unrepresented applicants fail in their attempts to secure a registration. Every single line on a trademark application is loaded with legal significance, which is frequently unrecognized. Most business owners shouldn't try to file their own trademark application any more than they should file their own business taxes, run their own payroll, or learn HTML to build their own website.

It is no longer 1995. You do not need to search for a local attorney, drive downtown, and meet with a $700-an-hour, grey flannel suit-wearing lawyer to get competent legal advice. There are multiple non-traditional, online-first law firms that specialize in trademark law. They can help you avoid making expensive mistakes, usually for just a few hundred dollars, and you can spend more of your time running your business. Because U.S. trademarks are governed by federal law, these online lawyers don't even need to be licensed or live in your state (or country).

The purpose of this book is to help you, the busy business person, identify those things that you don't know about trademark law that you need to know early, before you attempt to launch a brand name publicly.

Once informed, you will make better decisions about protecting your brands. You will avoid getting ripped off or taken advantage of. You will save valuable time and money.

Executive Summary

Your brand is your business's lifeline, and *U.S. Trademark Law for Busy Entrepreneurs* shows you how to protect it without getting lost in legal complexity. Tailored for startups and small businesses, this book simplifies U.S. trademark law into actionable steps to safeguard your identity and save you time and money.

Key insights include:

- **Why Federal Registration Matters**: Unlock powerful rights like federal court access, nationwide protection, and the ability to block infringers—affordable insurance for your brand.
- **Timing Is Everything**: File early—ideally before launching—to secure your rights and avoid costly rebranding down the road.

- **Choosing a Strong Mark**: Learn what makes a trademark distinctive and protectable, steering clear of generic or weak names.
- **Avoiding Pitfalls**: Sidestep scams, navigate USPTO refusals, and dodge infringement risks with smart strategies.
- **The Registration Process**: Master the steps, from searches to responding to challenges, with practical tips to keep things moving.
- **Maintaining Your Rights**: Keep your trademark alive with simple upkeep and enforcement know-how.
- **Going Global**: Use your U.S. registration to expand internationally via the Madrid System, plus insights for non-U.S. businesses entering the American market.
- **Free Resources**: Tap into tools like USPTO databases and free attorney-led trademark searches to support your journey.

Whether you're launching a startup or scaling globally, this guide equips you with the knowledge to protect your brand confidently. It's trademark law made simple—letting you focus on growing your business while keeping your most valuable asset secure.

* * *

Chapter 1
Why Bother? Benefits of Federal Trademark Registration

There is no legal requirement that you register your trademark anywhere. However, registering your trademarks is incredibly inexpensive insurance and gives you powerful rights. Among other things:

- You can legally use the ®, which warns potential infringers that the brand is officially registered and taken seriously by the owner.
- Trademark owners have access to the U.S. federal courts, which can issue injunctions against infringers and order payment of damages and attorney fees.
- Registered trademarks appear in the U.S. Trademark Office's online database. This database is searched by new businesses and trademark attorneys alike when considering the adoption of a new brand. Registration presents notice of your use of the trademark

and reduces the risk that a new competitor will try to adopt a similar name.

- The USPTO will stop new applicants from registering trademarks identical and similar to your own when they review new trademark applications, stopping infringers early (and at no cost to you beyond the cost of originally registering your trademark).

- Third parties will frequently enforce trademark rights without intervention of the courts. For example, third parties like Apple and Google will frequently take down infringing software from their app stores. Amazon will not allow other sellers to register or sell competing products under the same brand once a seller has registered for the Amazon Brand Registry (which requires a trademark registration).

- U.S. Customs will search for and stop infringing and counterfeit products at U.S. ports if the mark is registered with them for a small fee.

- Trademark registrations are business assets with titles, like real estate or vehicles. The title to each trademark registration can be assigned to a new owner, licensed, or used as collateral. If you ever sell your business, having clear title and ownership of your trademarks will likely help you fetch a higher price.

- If you find an infringer, sending a Cease and Desist letter for a registered trademark will be taken more seriously (see "access to U.S. federal courts" above).
- Taking the time to register your trademark will reduce the risk of your business being accused of trademark infringement. Securing a trademark registration means your trademark application was approved by the USPTO only after the trademark examining attorney found no registered trademarks similar to your own.
- U.S. trademark registrations can be used to extend your trademark rights to most other countries of the world via the World Intellectual Property Organization once your business grows globally.

For not a great deal of money, registering your trademarks helps to ensure that you are not an infringer, provides your business with powerful judicial and non-judicial enforcement tools, and provides tangible rights to your business that can be sold or transferred to others.

* * *

Chapter 2

When Should I Start Registering My Trademarks?

While we are biased, we advise clients to file trademark applications as soon as you believe you are going to launch a product or service. This is step number one, before you buy a domain, pay for graphic design, or spend tens of thousands of dollars filling your garage with inventory. In an ideal world, you would file your application 6-8 months in advance of launching your product or service, simply because the trademark office is slow in reviewing new applications and giving feedback on the likelihood that they will allow your trademark to register.

Wait a second - isn't it more expensive to file a trademark application before you have started using it to sell your products and services? Absolutely. It's going to add a few hundred dollars or more to your total cost, spread out in multiple payments over a year or more. Filing this way, you will need to file proof that you are using the trademark in U.S.

commerce and possibly one or more 6-month extensions of time. This adds some additional filings and fees compared to filing an application after you have started your business. Are we being greedy lawyers by offering this advice to our clients? You decide.

Several times a month we get the following phone call from prospective clients:

> "Hi Markavo, I'm calling to see if you can help me with a trademark refusal. I own my trademark. I've been in business for the last year now. I've got thousand of customers, lots of followers on Facebook, and I just spent a ton of money on new inventory. I filed my own trademark application about 6 months ago and I just received a letter from the trademark office saying that I can't register it because they found something they say is too similar. It seems sort of ridiculous. The trademarks aren't even the same. I searched the trademark office before I filed and didn't see the trademark they're talking about."

"OK. Let's take a look. Unfortunately, this seems like a reasonable refusal. Trademarks don't have to be identical, only similar. If the ideas presented by the trademarks are close to one another conceptually and the goods and services are competitive, like this case, it's unlikely that we could convince the trademark office that your mark should register. While there is a spelling difference and the other mark has a generic word on the end that yours doesn't, we really have little to write about that is supported by the law. Both companies are selling similar products and the marks present nearly identical ideas. If we argued this case we would probably lose. This is one we would have told you not to file had we been hired to clear it 6 months ago."

"That doesn't seem fair, like I said, I searched the trademark office using their online TESS search before I filed. This mark wasn't there."

"That's a pretty common complaint and unfortunately it's not a defence. A lot of people think searching for a trademark is like searching for a domain name. If they don't find anything identical, then it's available. However, that's not how it works. You have to find every similar trademark and the TESS search does not do that work for you automatically. You need to know specialized commands and syntax to use the government's search effectively. The trademark examiners just don't perform one search, they perform multiple searches, sometime five or more trying to find similar trademarks. Most private attorneys spend thousands of dollars a year on commercial trademark search software since the free TESS tool is so cumbersome to use."

"Well this sucks. What a waste of money. I guess I just won't register my trademark. I don't really need the registration anyway and I'll just keep doing what I've been doing."

"Before you do that, it's not so simple. It looks like the other company started using their trademark in the U.S. several years before you and secured their federal trademark not long after that. You need to be concerned about potential trademark infringement lawsuits. You sent in this application, received this refusal letter, and now you have been officially informed of their rights. The other company hasn't noticed you yet, but they may in the future. When they do you'll be considered a "knowing infringer" and that's when federal courts get cranky and award things like your profits, damages, and attorneys fees to the other company. There is a huge amount of legal and financial risk in ignoring this problem."

"But I've spent so much money on this company, I couldn't possibly change the name ...."

You don't want to have the above conversation with us or another trademark attorney and definitely not opposing trademark counsel. It's worth a few hundred extra dollars in government fees (and if you're using a lawyer, legal fees) to ensure you don't run into the above situation. What's a few hundred extra dollars in comparison to the expense of having to scrap a bunch of inventory, rework all your graphic design, lose momentum in your online SEO and social media marketing campaigns, and notify all of your customers of your re-branding (with many of them not noticing your notifications and not finding your new company).

Filing early not only will help ensure that you avoid wasting money on an easily avoidable re-brand, but also has the positive effect of ensuring that no one can adopt an identical or similar name while you prepare to launch your business. Your federal trademark rights date back to the day you filed an application, so even if it takes you three years or more to finally secure your registration, you're protected even before you get your first paying customer.

Everyone who files a similar or identical trademark application will be blocked by your pending application. You are first in line for your brand name at the trademark office provided you keep your application in good standing by filing all the necessary extensions of time and ultimately file proof that you have launched your brand and have made sales of your products and services to U.S. consumers.

* * *

Chapter 3

6 Things You Need to Understand Before Paying For Trademark Applications

The U.S. has some of the strictest trademark requirements in the world. The vast majority of the information submitted with a trademark application is chiseled in stone and can't be edited once filed. It presently takes upwards of half a year for the trademark office to first review your application and issue any potential refusals to register. Moreover, government filing fees (currently $350 per class) are not refundable, even if you made an honest mistake (because, as mentioned earlier, most information in a trademark application cannot be edited). Accordingly, it is essential that you understand what you are up against and seek out advice as needed, before you throw away hundreds of dollars and waste months of time on something that may not be trademarkable.

1. If you are outside the U.S., a U.S. attorney is mandatory

Before you get too deep into this book, note that if you are a company or individual located outside the U.S. applying for a U.S. trademark, you cannot file anything with the USPTO yourself. You are required to hire a licensed U.S. attorney to represent you in everything. You won't be able to file your own application or even make a minor change like updating the company phone number or email address. While this increases your expenses a bit, this is in line with how most other trademark offices work throughout the world.

If you have a lot of trademarks to file, don't try to be clever and think that you can just rent a U.S. mailing address to get around this requirement. The USPTO constantly cross-checks trademark applicant and owner mailing addresses against known mail forwarding services using databases compiled by commercial data brokers. Further, if you're outside the U.S., you're probably going to have all sorts of difficulties passing the mandatory ID verification process required to log in and file any USPTO documents. Your personal data is verified by referencing U.S. credit reporting and government ID databases, which can't be faked. You'll probably get caught and have to hire a U.S. attorney anyway to unwind the mess. We constantly see foreign applicants getting caught up in an inquisition about where their business really is located by attentive USPTO trademark examiners. There's a ton of fraud around this issue and the USPTO is very aware of the problem and aggressively pursues it.

The point is that if you're a foreign trademark applicant, you don't need to master all the details and nuances in this book. Gain a high-level overview and let your U.S. attorney do the leg work (that's what you pay them for).

2. Don't get ripped off

Online advertising, particularly paid search engine advertising on Google and Bing, is a cesspool of too-good-to-be-true $35 scams. Many of these sites advertised will simply take your money and run and will not file anything on your behalf. A large number of these companies have been shut down by law enforcement as they were run on behalf of organized crime overseas. These $35 services would bill the client for their service fees plus inflated "government fees" and never file anything with the USPTO. The "client" would be out thousands of dollars and not learn any different until months later. Notably absent from these sites is an indication of the attorneys or individuals responsible for performing the contracted-for services. These sites continue to pop up one after another as it's a highly profitable scam.

Keep in mind that the only parties the USPTO will grant a USPTO account to are licensed U.S. attorneys and U.S. businesses applying for or maintaining their own trademarks. If you're looking to avoid being scammed, ask for information about the attorney representing you and the state or U.S. territory they have a law license in. Filling out the trademark office forms alone can take upwards of an hour. None of the $35 scam sites are run by law firms or lawyers as it's not possible to search, clear, draft, and advise a client for $35 without losing your law license from multiple malpractice claims. Advertisements for a $35 trademark application are about as reasonable as a dentist advertising $100 braces for your kid. Something should seem off to you.

If you want to avoid being scammed, work with a licensed attorney. Even LegalZoom, a service made famous for paralegals filling out forms to save you money, now only offers trademark attorney-filed applications for over $500 in legal fees. There's no more "do it yourself with help" option because LegalZoom's form-filing paralegals can't file trademark documents anymore without having an attorney provide legal advice first.

The only options to file a U.S. trademark are to hire a licensed U.S. attorney or, as a business owner, file the applications yourself, unassisted, after validating your identity and opening a USPTO account.

Any other option is simply a scam.

3. What a trademark is

If you're going to try to file a trademark yourself or shop around for an attorney to hire, you need to have a basic understanding of what a trademark is.

Simply put, a trademark is a brand name of a product or service. It serves as a "source indicator" in the market so that consumers can quickly recognize what company or individual is behind a product or service. As a consumer, you know that TOYOTA builds reliable, long-lasting, affordable sedans. Toyota Motor Company is selling a product - a physical vehicle that consumers purchase and take delivery of. You know as a consumer that the car or truck you purchased is made by Toyota as the words are printed on the vehicle. The same principle applies to any other physical good - the brand name needs to be emblazoned on the product itself or its packaging so that the consumer makes the connection between the product they purchased and the brand name.

In the realm of services, STARBUCKS provides a relatively uniform coffee shop service experience across thousands of locations spread across the globe. Running a retail coffee shop is a service consisting of renting a retail space, filling it with knowledgeable employees, and keeping the coffee flowing throughout the day. As a consumer, you know who is responsible for providing the service as the name is on the sign on the door.

Accordingly, applying for a trademark is in some ways fairly mechanical. The applicant must first provide the brand to be registered (like a logo design or a wordmark like NIKE RUN CLUB). The applicant must then state in ordinary English the products (like shoes) and/or the services (providing a website that allows you to post the distances of your latest runs) that the application will cover.

What this means practically is that most businesses have multiple trademark registrations. Using Starbucks Inc. as an example again, they have over 400 trademarks. The majority of these registrations and applications are for the words STARBUCKS or their famous logo. The registrations and applications only differ in the products or services they cover.

4. What a trademark isn't

Not an invention or method

A trademark can never be an idea or an invention or a method. Trademarks only protect brand names of products or services. A competitor could come along and completely copy your idea, invention, or method in meticulous detail, and provided they called it something else, trademark law wouldn't help. While you invented the world's greatest waterless laundry detergent, SUPER SUDS, it does not mean your neighbor couldn't also go into the waterless laundry detergent business. All they would need to do is copy your idea but adopt a dissimilar brand like DRY BUBBLEZ. Ideas aren't protected by trademark law, brands are. Your neighbor would end up with trademark infringement headaches if they called their product something confusingly similar like ZUPER SUDZ, though, which is why you want to register your trademarks.

Not a "word or phrase" you "used first"

A trademark won't allow you to "own a word." Registering a trademark doesn't remove the word from the English language so that only you may use it.

While trademark registration provides exclusive rights to your brand, the protection is limited in scope to the products and services you actually provide to your customers. Thus, identical trademarks can be registered by different companies where the products and services don't compete in the marketplace. For example, DELTA is owned by Delta Airlines, covering "airline services," while DELTA is also registered by Moen Inc. covering "kitchen fixtures and faucets."

You could probably come along tomorrow and apply to protect DELTA for a "series of children's books" for the same reason. The ordinary consumer is unlikely to be confused by the identical brand name given that airline services, plumbing fixtures, and a children's book series are not products and services typically offered by the same company.

Not a domain name or social media account

You just spent $10,000 on greatdomain.com. However, there's no business there. You aren't selling products using the brand GREAT DOMAIN and you aren't selling services under the GREAT DOMAIN brand. What you own is a domain name, but because you aren't actively using it as a brand name of a product or service that has launched to the public yet, there's no trademark rights to be had.

Similarly, social media handles, by themselves, aren't eligible for trademark registration until they grow beyond simply posting, but rather build a business where they are advertising and selling goods or services using the brand.

In both of the above cases, it will make sense to get a trademark application filed early, based on your intent to use it in commerce in the future to preserve your rights while you prepare to launch your products and services in the marketplace. See chapter 2 for more information.

5. Commerce, Commerce, Commerce!

Before your trademark can register, it must be used in commerce in the United States.

Remember that trademark rights in the U.S. emerge out of the use of a brand name to advertise a good or service to consumers who then *purchase or use* the good or service. The purpose of trademark law is consumer protection as a brand of product or service gains a reputation for a certain level of quality. This whole structure of legal relations requires an ongoing business where the owners are spending time every day, every week, month after month promoting their offerings to consumers using their trademark.

There's no shortcut and no substitute to actually running a business to show use in commerce. Demonstrating "use in commerce" under the law, as opposed to what you think the common-sense definition of the phrase should be, can be expensive because it can take time.

Occasionally, you may have to pay for an extra extension of time or two. Because of this, clients always are looking for a loophole. Stop looking for a loophole, because there isn't one. Larger companies than yours have tried and failed.

What doesn't work? Here's an incomplete list of shenanigans we have seen:

- Arranging sham sales to Mom, a friend, or a neighbour, all made for the purpose of being able to say you made a sale instead of actually having real clients and customers.
- Trying to claim sales from a related business you already run, that uses completely different branding, as customers of the new trademark and new brand name.

- Ordering the tiniest amount of inventory, selling a few units on Facebook or eBay for the purpose of showing "use in commerce," then doing nothing to promote further sales for years.
- Trying to claim sales made entirely outside the U.S. by a related foreign entity as U.S. commerce.
- Creating realistic-looking computer-generated mock-ups of products that never existed and never were sold to anyone.
- Using the home office printer to ink-jet generic labels and suggesting that is your actual product sold to customers.
- Filing pictures found on the internet of some other company's product, claiming it as their own.
- Just plain old lying.

Who's going to know? Well, it's quite possible that you make it through the registration process and walk away with a registration certificate. This is an approach some choose to take, although unethical and illegal. No attorney will knowingly help you in this approach, though, as they risk their law license. But even ignoring morality, at a practical level, this rosy state of affairs with an ill-gotten registration will rapidly deteriorate as soon as there is a trademark dispute.

Real use in commerce generates a paper record that can't be faked. Think of the number of emails any legitimate business generates daily from the sales of goods or services - price quotes, invoices, merchant account transactions, receipts from vendors, correspondence between employees, contractors, and suppliers, and on and on. All of the above are dated and time-stamped and can be verified and cross-referenced against other evidence without much effort.

During a trademark dispute, you're going to be expected to produce copies of all of the above and more by opposing counsel. If you claimed you started using your trademark in commerce on date X, but can't provide documents establishing that you ordered supplies or provided price quotes or charged a client or customer's credit card on or before that use-in-commerce date, you are going to lose.

> "Pro-tip: Want to avoid tens of thousands in legal fees during litigation? Shut down document discovery before it even begins. Keep every email related to the adoption of your trademark and early use that supports the use-in-commerce date you claim on your trademark application. Be conservative in selecting the date and make sure you have a pile of convincing evidence supporting your use-in-commerce date to show opposing counsel should a trademark dispute emerge.

Do you really want the future of your trademark to hinge on a single email about a single sale?"

There is no requirement that your business be successful to be eligible for trademark protection. However, it does require, especially early on, that your promotional efforts are continuous and your sales reflect that effort. "Token sales" once or twice a year to secure a trademark registration, lying, or other low-effort approaches will ultimately fail and your trademark will be deemed invalid or abandoned. Because of the evidentiary requirements, trying to claim "use in commerce" of your trademark too early to save a few bucks is a waste of your time and money. What point is there to this whole exercise if all you end up with is an indefensible, unenforceable "registration"?

6. Litigation is the Sport of Kings

What's at stake with a carelessly drafted trademark application? Imagine that a trademark dispute emerges with a third party after you have been in the market for several years; you lose or are threatened with financial ruin by a more powerful opponent and must rebrand.

In some countries, having a trademark registration certificate is all the magic you need to win in a trademark dispute. Walk into the courtroom, wave your paper around, and your claim of trademark infringement is granted. You were, after all, the first to register your trademark, so of course you should win.

The U.S., though, doesn't award trademark supremacy to the first party that manages to secure a registration at the trademark office. Instead, the party that has superior rights is the first to use their trademark in commerce in the United States *even without registering the trademark anywhere*. Even more troubling is the fact that one could have a registration that appears to support the claim of earlier use in commerce, but it is in fact indefensible as the original trademark applicant misunderstood an important legal concept or misstated some important fact. In the U.S., it's the truth that matters - the facts, evidence, and declarations supporting your claims of use in commerce must all align. If they don't, then you're in trouble.

There are tens of thousands of U.S. trademark registrations granted every year that are worthless legally as they were procured either by trademark office oversight, applicant fraud, or honest mistake. Just because a trademark examiner missed something isn't a defense. Just because you didn't understand an important legal concept and "filled out the application wrong" won't save the day either. The USPTO doesn't perform a deep-dive investigation of the claims you make. They assume the sworn declarations that the trademark applicant makes are true and that the applicant really understood the legal concepts they were making declarations about. If the application looks good superficially and meets the checkbox list of statutory requirements, a registration will be granted. It's the old saying "garbage in, garbage out." Unfortunately, many businesses only learn about how complicated this area of law is years after they registered their trademarks when a trademark dispute emerges.

A typical way disputes emerge is that a user of a similar trademark to yours applies to register their own trademark. They get blocked by your trademark registration and they call a trademark attorney who advises them on all the ways they can potentially cancel or limit the scope of your trademark registration.

If a party files to have your trademark canceled, for example, the proceeding is governed by procedural rules that are nearly identical to those used in a federal lawsuit. Unless you want to spend hour upon hour researching how this or that type of brief or motion is filed and how to undertake effective discovery of evidence and testimony, you're going to spend tens of thousands of dollars or more on experienced trademark counsel.

Your goals as a business owner should be first to ensure that you aren't using a trademark that is confusingly similar to another. Then you need to make sure you completely understand what is required for a successful, iron-clad trademark application or hire someone who already knows.

Trademark disputes are lengthy, expensive, and generally a waste of time and money. Do some risk management in evaluating potential conflicts before you file and make sure you deeply understand what you have signed before clicking "submit" on that online trademark application form.

* * *

.

Chapter 4

What Makes a Good Trademark?

Picking a trademark is like naming your kid—it's got to stand out, stick in people's heads, and hold up under pressure. But here's the catch: not every name is a winner. Some are legal duds, while others are branding superstars. The secret lies in something called the "spectrum of distinctiveness." Let's dive in and figure out how to pick a name that'll make your business shine—and keep the lawyers off your back.

Understanding the Spectrum of Distinctiveness

Imagine trademark strength as a ladder. The higher you climb, the tougher and more protectable your mark becomes. Here's the rundown, rung by rung:

Generic Marks (Bottom Rung)

These are plain-Jane words like "phone" for a phone company or "bread" for a bakery. They're about as useful as a ladder with no rungs—zero protection. Why? Because you can't own a word everyone needs to describe their stuff. "Coffee" for a coffee shop? Nope. The USPTO will shut that down faster than you can say "latte."

Descriptive Marks (Next Rung)

These tell it like it is—like FAST SHIPPING for a delivery service or SOFT for a pillow brand. They're a step up, but still shaky. You *might* get them trademarked, but only if you've already made a name for yourself (that's "secondary meaning" in legal-speak). Even then, they're wobbly—think of a ladder that creaks under pressure.

Suggestive Marks (Middle Rung)

Now we're talking. These hint at what you do without spilling the beans. NETFLIX suggests "internet movies," but doesn't say it outright. They're inherently distinctive—no fame required—and ready to protect from day one. This is your sturdy, reliable ladder.

Arbitrary Marks (Higher Rung)

These are wild cards—common words used in unexpected ways. APPLE for computers? PENGUIN for books? No obvious link, which makes them stand out and tough to copy. They're the rock-solid steel ladders of trademarks.

Fanciful Marks (Top Rung)

The VIPs of the trademark world: made-up words like KODAK or XEROX. They've got no meaning until you give them one, making them the titanium ladders—sleek, strong, and nearly unbeatable.

Why It Matters

The higher your mark sits on this ladder, the easier it is to lock down and defend. Generic and descriptive marks are a slog (if they're even possible), but suggestive, arbitrary, and fanciful marks? They're your fast track to a trademark that works as hard as you do. Less time in court, more time building your empire.

Why Suggestive or Arbitrary Trademarks Make Good Business Sense

A great trademark isn't just about dodging legal traps—it's about building a brand that pops. Suggestive and arbitrary marks are the MVPs here, and here's why they're worth your time:

Cut Through the Noise

In a sea of "TechTrend" and "ProService" snoozers, names like APPLE or INSTAGRAM grab attention. Arbitrary marks (like APPLE for computers) and suggestive ones (like INSTAGRAM for instant photo and video sharing) are memorable because they're different. They're the neon sign in a grey crowd.

Lock It Down Easy

These marks are legal powerhouses. Their uniqueness makes them harder to challenge, whether it's the USPTO or a competitor sniffing around. AMAZON for an online store beats SHOPONLINE every time—less hassle, more protection.

Hook Your Customers

Suggestive marks like NETFLIX tease what's on offer without boring anyone. They spark curiosity—think of them as a trailer for your brand. People lean in, wanting to know more.

Build a Vibe

Names like INSTAGRAM don't just describe—they *evoke a feeling*. Instant, visual, and connected. That emotional hook turns customers into fans, and fans stick around.

Future-Proof Your Brand

These marks give you wiggle room. GOOGLE started as a search engine—now it's phones, car software, you name it. If they'd gone with SEARCH QUICK, they'd be stuck. A flexible name grows with you, no rebrand required.

The Takeaway: A suggestive or arbitrary trademark isn't just a legal win—it's a business edge. It's your brand's personality, protection, and potential, all rolled into one.

Wrapping It Up

Your trademark isn't just a name—it's your brand's backbone. Aim for suggestive, arbitrary, or fanciful marks to get a head start on protection, buzz, and growth. Get creative, test your ideas, and pick something that'll carry you far.

* * *

Chapter 5
Performing Trademark Searches

Picture this: you've got a killer brand name, you've ordered inventory, and your logo's already on business cards. Then—bam—six months later, the trademark office says, "Nope, too confusing with someone else's mark." You're out hundreds (maybe thousands) of dollars, stuck with useless stock, and back to square one. All because you skipped a proper trademark search. Sound like a nightmare? It happens more than you'd think.

Here's the cold truth: the top reason trademarks get shot down is "likelihood of confusion." That's when your name's too close to someone else's, and customers might mix you up. You don't find that out until the USPTO reviews your application—six months of waiting, wasted fees, and a big fat rejection. A solid search upfront can save you from that mess.

But don't kid yourself—trademark searches aren't like snagging a domain name. It's not about exact matches. It's about sniffing out *similar* marks that could trip you up. Most DIY-ers miss this and end up with false hope—or a legal headache.

The Legal Stuff, Made Simple

There's a fancy list called the *DuPont* factors—13 of them—that the trademark office uses to figure out if two marks are too close. Don't worry, you won't need to crack a law book. Here's the gist:

- **Do the marks look or sound alike?** PEAKPULSE vs. PEAKPLUS? Trouble.
- **Are you in the same game?** Both selling workout gear? Bigger trouble.
- **Could customers get mixed up?** If they might think your stuff comes from the other guy, you're toast.

That's the core of it. Sure, there's more—like how famous the other mark is—but these three are the heavy hitters. Miss them, and you're betting your brand on luck.

Knockout Searches: Your Quick Gut Check

A knockout search is your first move—like peeking at your poker hand before going all in. It's fast, cheap, and spots the obvious dealbreakers. Think identical or near-identical marks in your industry. BREWBUDDY for your coffee shop when there's a BREWBUDDY tea brand? Dead in the water.

Here's the playbook:

- **Jump into the USPTO database -** (TESS if you're nerdy).
- **Search your mark**—exact hits or close cousins.
- **Check the classes**—same turf (like food and drink)? Bad news.

Find a match? Ditch the name and move on. Nothing pops up? You're not safe yet, but you've cleared the first hurdle.

> **Pro Tip**: Knockouts are perfect for killing dumb ideas fast. They're not the whole story, but they'll keep you from face-planting early. Don't want to do this yourself? Markavo® offers free knockout searches performed by trademark attorneys.

Common Law Searches: The Deep Dive

Now it gets real. Even if a mark isn't registered with the USPTO, someone could still own it under "common law"—aka they've been using it in business without filing the paperwork. Those unregistered marks can still sink your ship or drag you into court.

A common law search means rolling up your sleeves:

- **State business registrations**—every state's got one.
- **Business directories**—Google, Yelp, you name it.
- **Online turf**—domains, social media, anywhere your name might pop up.
- **Industry corners**—trade mags, forums, or even Amazon.

It's a grind, but it's your shield against surprises. Say you're launching FITFUEL protein bars. A knockout search is clean, but a common law dig finds a gym slinging FITFUEL shakes. That gym could ruin your day—especially if they've got years on you.

Why a Pro's Worth It

Let's not sugarcoat it: trademark law is a beast. The USPTO's rulebook is 1,500 pages of dense legalese. You're not cracking that between coffee runs. A trademark attorney isn't just a luxury—they're your lifeline.

What you get:

- **X-ray vision**: They spot risks you'd breeze past.
- **Time back**: You run your business; they wrestle the search.
- **Plan B**: If your mark's shaky, they'll tweak it or save it.

It's not cheap, but it's cheaper than a rebrand—or a lawsuit. Think of it as investing in peace of mind and a bulletproof brand.

Wrap It Up

Trademark searches aren't glamorous, but they're non-negotiable. Start with a knockout to ditch the flops fast. Follow with a common law sweep to catch the sneaky stuff. And if you're serious about your business, hire a pro to keep the wolves at bay.

* * *

Chapter 6
Strategizing – What Should Be Filed First?

Trademark protection is a vital investment in your brand's future, especially for startups and small businesses with limited resources. Strategizing your trademark filings is all about maximizing protection while managing costs and time effectively. A well-planned approach ensures that your most valuable brand assets are secured first, giving your business a strong legal foundation as it grows and reducing the risk of costly disputes later.

For busy entrepreneurs, the key is to prioritize filings in a way that offers the broadest and most essential protection upfront, then builds on that foundation as your brand evolves. The recommended approach is straightforward: **file the wordmark of your main brand name first**, followed by **your company logo**, and then **any taglines or names of important products or services**. This order leverages the strengths of each type of trademark to create comprehensive protection, starting with the core of your brand—its name—and then adding the visual and supplementary elements that make it unique.

Filing the Wordmark First

Definition of a Wordmark

A wordmark is the text-only version of your trademark —your brand name stripped of any graphical elements, designs, or specific stylization. It's the simplest form of your brand's identity, focusing solely on the words themselves. When you register a wordmark, you're protecting the name in any way it's presented, whether in plain text, a fancy font, or alongside a logo. This flexibility makes it a powerful tool for safeguarding your brand.

Examples:

- **COCA COLA**: Just the words, no specific design attached.
- **GOOGLE**: The name alone, regardless of how it's styled.
- **NIKE**: A simple text mark that covers the brand name universally.

These examples show how a wordmark focuses on the essence of the brand—the name—without tying it to a particular visual representation.

Why It Provides the Broadest Protection

Filing the wordmark first is the cornerstone of a smart trademark strategy because it offers the widest scope of legal protection. Here's why:

- **Foundation of Your Brand**: The wordmark secures your brand name across all its uses— whether it's in marketing materials, on product packaging, or incorporated into a logo. It's the bedrock of your trademark portfolio, ensuring that the heart of your identity is protected no matter how it's displayed. For a startup or small business, this broad coverage is critical because it establishes your claim to the name early on.
- **Blocks Similar Names**: Registering the wordmark prevents competitors from using names that are confusingly similar, even if their logos or designs differ. The U.S. Patent and Trademark Office (USPTO) and courts focus on whether marks could confuse consumers, and a wordmark gives you leverage to stop others from encroaching on your brand's name. For example, if you register PEAKPULSE as a wordmark for fitness gear, you could challenge a competitor using PEAKPULSE PRO for similar products, regardless of their logo.
- **Versatility**: Since a wordmark isn't tied to a specific design or style, it offers unmatched

flexibility. You can update your logo, change your branding colors, or tweak your marketing without needing to file a new trademark application, as long as the name stays the same. This adaptability is a huge advantage for growing businesses that might evolve their look over time.

In short, the wordmark acts like a legal shield, covering your brand name in its purest form and giving you the most bang for your buck when resources are tight.

Filing the Company Logo Next

Definition of a Logo Trademark

A logo trademark protects the visual design of your brand. This can include graphical elements (like symbols or icons), stylized text (like a unique font), or a combination of both. Unlike a wordmark, which is text-only, a logo trademark locks down the specific artistic representation of your brand that consumers see and recognize. It's about safeguarding the "face" of your business—the image that sets you apart visually.

Examples:

- **Nike swoosh**: A simple, iconic symbol with no text.

- **Starbucks logo**: The mermaid and the blocky font present unique ideas that are separate from the words "Starbucks Coffee."

These logos are more than just pretty designs—they're powerful identifiers that complement the brand name.

How It Complements the Wordmark

Filing your company logo after the wordmark builds on the foundation you've already established. Here's how the two work together:

- **Visual Protection**: While the wordmark secures your brand name, the logo trademark protects the specific visual identity that consumers associate with your business. For example, if someone tries to copy your logo but uses a slightly different name, you can still enforce your rights based on the logo registration. This adds a layer of protection against imitators who might try to mimic your brand's look and feel.
- **Holistic Coverage**: Together, the wordmark and logo trademark create a comprehensive shield around your brand's identity. The wordmark covers the name in any form, while the logo trademark locks down the exact design and over all style you use. This

combination leaves little room for competitors to imitate your brand without stepping on your legal toes. For instance, a rival couldn't use a logo similar to yours *and* a name close to yours without risking infringement on both fronts.

- **Consumer Recognition**: Logos often play a huge role in how customers identify your brand—think of the Nike swoosh on a shoe or the Apple logo on a laptop. Protecting your logo ensures that the visual elements that make your brand stand out are legally yours. For small businesses, where every customer impression counts, this can be a game-changer.

By filing the logo trademark second, you're reinforcing the wordmark's protection and securing the visual elements that make your brand memorable.

Filing Taglines and Product/Service Names

Definition of Taglines and Product/Service Names

Beyond your main brand name and logo, there are other elements worth protecting as your business grows:

- **Taglines**: These are catchy phrases or slogans tied to your brand that often convey its message or values. They're memorable hooks that stick in customers' minds, like Nike's JUST DO IT.

- **Product/Service Names**: These are the distinct names you give to your key offerings, such as Apple's IPHONE or Uber's UBER EATS. They identify specific products or services under your broader brand umbrella.

Both taglines and product/service names can become valuable assets as your brand gains traction.

Why They Are Important to Protect

While they're not as foundational as your wordmark or logo, taglines and product/service names deserve attention because:

- **Marketing Power**: Taglines shape how customers perceive your brand and create an emotional connection. A strong tagline like JUST DO IT becomes synonymous with Nike's ethos of determination and action. Protecting it ensures competitors can't steal that messaging power or dilute it with similar phrases.

- **Product Identity**: Unique product or service names distinguish your offerings in a crowded market. The IPHONE name, for example, sets Apple's smartphone apart from generic "smartphones." Without protection, others could use similar names, confusing customers or piggybacking on your success.

- **Risk of Loss**: If you don't register these elements, competitors could adopt similar taglines or product names, weakening your brand's distinctiveness. Imagine a rival launching a phone called IPHONIC — without a trademark, you'd have a harder time stopping them. Protecting these assets preserves your brand's clarity and reputation.

For startups and small businesses, these additional filings come into play as you expand your offerings or marketing efforts, making them a smart follow-up to the core wordmark and logo.

Conclusion

Summary of the Strategy

To build a strong trademark portfolio that protects your brand effectively, follow this prioritized strategy:

- 1. **File the Wordmark First**: Start with your brand name in its simplest form for the broadest protection. It's the foundation that secures your identity across all uses and blocks similar names.
- 2. **File the Logo Next**: Add protection for your brand's visual design, complementing the wordmark and safeguarding the look that customers recognize.

- 3. **File Taglines and Product/Service Names Last**: Secure these additional elements—memorable phrases and specific offering names—once your core identity is locked down.

This approach ensures your most critical assets are protected first, giving you a solid base to grow from while managing costs and complexity.

Practical Tips

- **File Early**: In trademark law, priority matters. Filing sooner rather than later establishes your rights and reduces the chance of someone else claiming a similar mark first. For startups, this means filing as soon as you're committed to a brand name—ideally before you launch (see Chapter 2 for more on timing).
- **Budget Wisely**: If money's tight, focus on the wordmark first. It's the most essential and cost-effective step, offering the widest protection for a single filing fee (typically $350 per class at the USPTO). You can add the logo and other elements later as revenue grows.
- **Seek Legal Advice**: Trademark law is full of nuances — likelihood of confusion, proper classifications, and filing requirements can

trip up even savvy entrepreneurs. A trademark attorney can ensure your applications are accurate and strategically sound, saving you from costly mistakes. For a few hundred dollars, it's an investment that pays off in peace of mind and protection.

By following this strategy and keeping these tips in mind, you'll protect your brand efficiently and effectively, setting your business up for success without breaking the bank or drowning in legal complexity.

* * *

Chapter 7

The U.S. Trademark Registration Process

Registering a trademark is a critical step in safeguarding your brand, but it's not a quick fix or a simple task. It's a multi-step journey that can span several months to over a year, depending on factors like the complexity of your application and any challenges that arise. For busy entrepreneurs, understanding the U.S. trademark registration process is vital because it equips you to prepare effectively, sidestep unnecessary delays, and secure the legal protection your brand needs to stand out and succeed.

Think of this process as constructing a house. You wouldn't start building without a solid plan, and likewise, you shouldn't jump into trademark registration without knowing what lies ahead. Each phase—from researching your mark before filing to maintaining your registration after approval— demands careful attention and timely action. A misstep, like missing a deadline or misinterpreting a requirement, could cost you time, money, or even your trademark rights.

This chapter offers a clear, high-level guide to the entire U.S. trademark registration process, tailored for startups and small business owners who may not have a legal background. We'll break it down into digestible sections: pre-filing considerations, the application process, examination and potential hurdles, publication and opposition, and finally, registration and ongoing maintenance. Whether you're just brainstorming your brand or ready to file, this roadmap will help you navigate with confidence.

Pre-Filing Considerations

Before you even touch a trademark application, there are essential steps to take to ensure your mark is ready for registration. These pre-filing considerations are the foundation of a successful application—they help confirm your trademark is protectable, unique, and strategically aligned with your business goals.

Conducting a Trademark Search

Why it's essential: A trademark search is your first shield against future trouble. It checks whether your desired mark is unique and doesn't overlap with existing trademarks, reducing the risk of rejection by the U.S. Patent and Trademark Office (USPTO) or legal disputes down the line. Imagine launching your brand only to discover someone else already owns the trademark—it's like buying a car without checking the title. A search helps you avoid that nightmare. See Chapter 5 to review trademark searches in depth.

Types of searches:

- **Knockout search**: This is a fast, initial scan to spot obvious conflicts. You can do it yourself using the USPTO's Trademark Electronic Search System (TESS) to see if identical or very similar marks are already registered in your industry. It's a great starting point but won't catch everything. Markavo® will also perform a knockout search for you for free and provide attorney feedback on the results.

- **Comprehensive search**: This is a thorough investigation that goes beyond the federal database. It covers state trademark registrations, unregistered (common law) marks in use, business names, domain names, and even social media handles. It's like hiring a detective to uncover any potential threats to your mark.

> **Pro tip**: You can possibly handle a knockout search on your own if you take the time to learn the rules about likelihood of confusion, but a comprehensive search is more intricate and worth the investment. Hiring a trademark attorney or a professional search firm ensures you get a detailed report and expert analysis,

minimizing the chance of surprises—like a costly rebrand or lawsuit—later on.

Understanding Trademark Types

Your trademark isn't just your brand name—it's how your customers recognize you, and there are different ways to protect it.

- **Wordmarks**: These protect the text of your brand name, without any specific design or styling. Examples include COCA COLA or AMAZON. Wordmarks offer broad protection because they cover the name itself, no matter how it's displayed.
- **Design marks (logos)**: These safeguard visual elements, like a logo or stylized text. Think of Starbucks' mermaid or McDonald's golden arches. Protection is tied to that specific design, so if you tweak it significantly, you might need a new registration.
- **Other types**: Beyond names and logos, you can register taglines (e.g., THINK DIFFERENT by Apple), product names (e.g., BIG MAC), or even non-traditional marks like sounds (e.g., MGM's lion roar), colors (e.g., UPS brown), or scents (though these are rare and tough to register).

Why it matters: Picking the right type depends on what's most valuable to your brand. A wordmark is a smart starting point for broad name protection, but if your logo is iconic, you'll want to lock that down too. Understanding these options helps you build a protection strategy that fits your business. See Chapter 6 for a in-depth discussion of what you should register and when.

Choosing the Filing Basis

When you file, the USPTO needs to know whether you're already using your mark or planning to use it soon. This is your "filing basis," and it shapes your application's path.

- **Use in commerce**: Choose this if you're actively selling goods or services under your mark in the U.S. You'll need to submit proof— a "specimen"—like a product label, packaging, or a website screenshot showing the mark in action.
- **Intent to use**: Opt for this if you haven't launched yet but have a solid plan to use the mark soon. You won't need a specimen upfront, but you'll have to provide one later to finalize registration.
- **Foreign Application or Foreign Registration:** If your company is located outside the U.S., it's possible to file a U.S. application if you have a foreign application

or registration in some cases. You can't make any changes to the trademark, the listed goods or services, or the owner, but you will not need to immediately show use in commerce.

Why it matters: Your filing basis impacts your timeline and strategy. "Use in commerce" can speed things up since you've already met the use requirement, while "intent to use" buys you time to roll out your brand while staking your claim at the USPTO. Either way, you'll eventually need to show use in commerce to get registered.

The Application Process

With your pre-filing work done, it's time to prepare and submit your application. This stage is all about precision—small errors can lead to big delays or outright rejection.

Key information required:

- **Applicant details**: Your legal name (or your business's legal name), address, and entity type (e.g., individual, LLC, corporation). Get this right—mistakes can create ownership issues later or even an invalid trademark registration.
- **Trademark details**: Specify if it's a wordmark, design mark, or other type. For

wordmarks, just enter the text. For design marks, upload a clear image. If you're filing "use in commerce," include a specimen showing the mark in use.

- **Goods and services**: Describe what you're selling or offering under the mark, sorted into USPTO classes (e.g., Class 9 for software, Class 25 for clothing). This defines your protection's scope, and you can't broaden it later without a new application. Attorney advice can go a long way in saving you time and money in regards to what you should cover.

Pro tip: Spend extra time on the goods and services description—it's the heart of your application. Use the USPTO's Acceptable Identification of Goods and Services Manual for guidance, or consult an attorney. A vague or sloppy description can weaken your protection or trigger a rejection.

Filing the Application

Submit online: TEAS is the fastest, cheapest way to file. Paper filings are an option but cost more and take longer.

Pay the filing fee: Fees depend on how many classes you're covering. In most cases, the government fees are $350 per international class. If your brand spans multiple categories (e.g., apparel and accessories), you'll pay $350 for each class.

Receive a serial number: After submission, the USPTO assigns a serial number—your application's tracking ID. Use it to check progress online.

> **Pro tip**: Save your serial number and set a reminder to monitor your application using the USPTO's Trademark Status and Document Retrieval (TSDR) tool. Staying proactive keeps you ahead of any issues.

Examination and Potential Challenges

Once filed, your application heads to the USPTO for review. This phase tests whether your mark meets legal standards—and it's where problems can surface.

Initial review: An examining attorney reviews your application 3-6 months after filing, checking for completeness and compliance with trademark rules. They'll assess if your mark is distinctive and free of conflicts.

Possible outcomes:

- **Approval**: If all's clear, your mark moves to publication.
- **Office Action**: If there's an issue, you'll get a formal notice—an Office Action—detailing problems like a refusal or a request for more info.

Office Actions

What is an Office Action?: It's a letter from the USPTO flagging issues with your application. You have three months to respond, or your application is abandoned. Chapter 8 provides a deeper dive into this topic.

Common refusal reasons:

- **Likelihood of confusion**: Your mark resembles an existing one, risking consumer mix-ups.
- **Descriptiveness**: Your mark just describes your product (e.g., "Fast" for delivery) and isn't unique enough.
- **Genericness**: Your mark is too common (e.g., "Shoes" for footwear) to be protectable.

How to respond: Address each point raised. You might:

- Argue why your mark is distinct or doesn't conflict.

- Submit evidence, like proof of use or acquired distinctiveness.
- Amend your application, such as refining the goods and services.

Pro tip: Office Actions are common, so don't panic. But they can get technical—especially with refusals like "likelihood of confusion." If it's tricky, hire an attorney to boost your chances of success.

Publication and Opposition

If your application passes examination, it's published for public review. This step invites scrutiny—and potential challenges—from others.

Publication in the Official Gazette

- **What happens**: Your mark appears in the USPTO's Official Gazette, a weekly online publication, for 30 days. It's a public announcement that your registration is nearing approval.
- **Why it matters**: This window lets third parties—like competitors—review your mark and object if they think it harms their rights by filing an opposition.

The Opposition Period

What is an opposition?: It's a formal challenge filed with the Trademark Trial and Appeal Board (TTAB) by someone claiming your mark infringes on theirs. It's like a courtroom showdown, with arguments and evidence from both sides.

How to handle it: If opposed, you'll need to defend your application before the TTAB. This can be time-consuming and expensive, often requiring legal help.

> **Pro tip**: Oppositions are rare (less than 3% of applications are opposed). Most applications go unchallenged. A strong pre-filing search reduces this risk. If one hits, act fast; missing deadlines can kill your application.

Registration and Post-Registration Maintenance

Clear the opposition hurdle, and you're almost done. But registration isn't the end—it's the start of keeping your trademark alive.

Issuance of the Registration Certificate

. . .

Final step: If no opposition arises (or you win one), the USPTO issues your certificate. For "use in commerce" filings, this takes about 10-12 weeks after the opposition period. For "intent to use," you'll need to submit proof of use first.

What it means: You're officially registered and can use the ® symbol, signalling nationwide protection and stronger enforcement rights.

Maintaining Your Registration

Why maintenance matters: Trademarks can last forever if you keep them active. Skip the upkeep, and your registration could be canceled.

See chapter 8 to understand the requirements of maintaining a registered trademark in depth.

Conclusion

The U.S. trademark registration process may feel overwhelming, but breaking it into steps makes it doable. Here's the rundown:

- 1. **Pre-filing**: Search for conflicts, pick your trademark type, and choose your filing basis ("use in commerce," "intent to use" or "foreign application or registration").

- 2. **Application**: Prepare and file via TEAS, nailing your goods and services description.
- 3. **Examination**: Wait for USPTO review and tackle any Office Actions within six months.
- 4. **Publication**: Survive the 30-day opposition window in the Official Gazette.
- 5. **Registration**: Get your certificate and maintain it with regular filings.

Key takeaways for busy entrepreneurs:

- **Start early**: Plan for 6-12 months—or more—if complications arise.
- **Be thorough**: Accuracy in your application prevents setbacks.
- **Stay engaged**: Track your status, respond promptly, and don't slack on maintenance.

With this knowledge, you're ready to protect your brand effectively. If the legal details get murky, a trademark attorney can be your safety net—saving you headaches and ensuring your trademark stands strong.

* * *

Chapter 8

Responding to Office Action Refusals

As a busy entrepreneur building your brand, you've taken the smart step of filing a trademark application with the United States Patent and Trademark Office (USPTO). But what happens when you receive an **Office Action**? Simply put, an Office Action is a formal notice from the USPTO sent during the examination of your trademark application. It's the examiner's way of saying, "We've found some issues or refusals that need to be addressed before your mark can be registered." These issues could be anything from a minor paperwork glitch to a major hurdle questioning whether your mark qualifies for protection.

Why does this matter? An Office Action isn't just a formality—it's a critical moment in the trademark process. How you respond can determine whether your mark gets approved or rejected. A strong response can clear the path to registration, protecting your brand and giving you exclusive rights to your mark. A weak response—or no response at all—can sink your application, leaving your brand vulnerable. For startups and small businesses, this is a big deal: your trademark is often tied to your identity, your reputation, and your competitive edge.

In this chapter, we'll break down everything you need to know about responding to an Office Action. We'll cover the **deadlines** you can't afford to miss, the **types of issues** you might face, and why bringing in **experienced trademark counsel** can be a game-changer for tricky cases. By the end, you'll have a roadmap to tackle an Office Action with confidence, even if you're new to the legal side of things.

Deadlines You Need to Know

The Three-Month Response Window

When the USPTO sends you an Office Action, they don't give you forever to reply. You have **three months** from the date the Office Action is issued to submit a full response. This isn't a suggestion—it's a hard deadline. The issuance date is typically stamped on the document, so check it carefully and mark your calendar.

What happens if you miss it? If you don't respond within those three months, your trademark application will be **abandoned**. That's a fancy way of saying it's game over for this application. You'll lose your filing fees, your original filing date (which determines your priority over other marks), and you'll have to start the entire process from scratch if you still want that trademark. For a small business, this could mean losing months of progress and opening the door for a competitor to swoop in with a similar mark.

Note procrastinators and the disorganized do get one more bite at the apple when a Notice of Abandonment is issued by the USPTO, allowing a late response to be filed within 2 months in exchange for $250 in late fees.

> **Pro tip**: Don't procrastinate. As soon as you get the Office Action, set multiple reminders—on your phone, your calendar, wherever works for you. Aim to get your response in well before the three-month mark. Unexpected delays (like gathering evidence or consulting an attorney) can sneak up on you, so starting early gives you breathing room.

Extensions: Limited Options

Hoping for a little extra time? You can extend the three month deadline by an additional three months by paying $125. You can do this only once.

> **Pro tip**: Treat the three-month deadline as set in stone. Build a plan to respond as soon as possible, and if you're juggling a busy

schedule, consider delegating or getting help to ensure it gets done.

Types of Possible Issues in Office Actions

An Office Action isn't a one-size-fits-all document. The issues it raises depend on your specific mark, your goods or services, and what's already in the USPTO's database. These issues fall into two main buckets: **substantive refusals** and **procedural issues**. Let's unpack each.

Substantive Refusals

Substantive refusals are the heavy hitters—they question whether your mark can even be registered. These are often the trickiest to overcome and may need some legal muscle to address. Here are the most common ones:

- **Likelihood of confusion**: The examiner thinks your mark is too similar to an existing registered trademark, and customers might mix them up. For example, if you're trying to register PEAKPULSE for fitness gear and there's already a PEAKPULSE for sports drinks, this could be a problem. The examiner looks at the marks' appearance, sound, meaning, and the relatedness of the goods or services.

- **Descriptiveness**: Your mark describes your goods or services too directly, making it hard to claim as uniquely yours. Think CREAMY YOGURT for a yogurt brand—it's clear what you're selling, but it's not distinctive enough unless you can prove customers associate it only with you (more on that later).
- **Genericness**: The mark is a common term anyone in your industry could use, like "Shoes" for a shoe company. Generic terms can't be trademarked because they don't identify a specific source—they're just the name of the product.
- **Other examples**: You might also hit roadblocks if your mark is:
- **Geographic**: Like TEXAZ BBQ for a barbecue joint in Texas—it's descriptive of where you're from.
- **A surname**: Like JOHNSON PLUMBING— surnames need extra proof of distinctiveness.
- **Ornamental**: Like a cool design on a T-shirt that's decorative but doesn't act as a brand identifier.

Pro tip: Substantive refusals can feel like a punch to the gut, but they're not always a dead end. Overcoming them often requires legal arguments or evidence, so don't wing it if you're unsure.

Procedural Issues

Procedural issues are less about your mark itself and more about the paperwork or technical details of your application. They're usually easier to fix but still need your attention. Examples include:

- **Classification errors**: The USPTO organizes trademarks into "classes" based on goods or services (e.g., Class 25 for clothing, Class 9 for electronics). If you put your app in Class 9 (hardware) when it should be Class 42 (software services), that's a classification error.
- **Specimen problems**: When you file, you submit a "specimen" showing your mark in use—like a photo of your product packaging or a screenshot of your website. If the specimen doesn't clearly show the mark, isn't in actual commerce, or doesn't match your application, the examiner will flag it.
- **Requests for clarification**: The examiner might need more info, like a clearer description of what you're selling or who owns the mark if it's a company name.

  Pro tip: These issues might seem minor, but ignoring them can stall your application. Double-check your filing details and be ready to tweak them as needed.

Variability of Issues

Here's the thing: no two Office Actions are identical. You might get one substantive refusal, a mix of procedural hiccups, or a laundry list of both. It all depends on your mark, what you're selling, and what's already registered. For instance, a simple logo for a coffee shop might sail through, while a descriptive name for a tech gadget might hit multiple snags.

> **Pro tip**: Don't skim the Office Action—read it line by line. Highlight every issue the examiner mentions, and if something's confusing, don't guess. Reach out to the examiner (their contact info is usually included) or get help to make sure you're clear on what's being asked.

Considerations

Now that you know what you're up against, how do you fight back? Responding to an Office Action is about being thorough, strategic, and timely. Here's how to approach it.

Basic Steps

No matter the issue, your response needs to cover all the bases:

- **Address everything**: The USPTO wants you to tackle **every single point** raised in the Office Action. If they list three issues and you only respond to two, your application could still be refused. Make a checklist of each concern and confirm you've covered them all.

- **Support your case**: Depending on the problem, you might need to:
  - **Make arguments**: Explain why the examiner's wrong—like showing your mark isn't confusingly similar to another.
  - **Submit evidence**: Provide proof, like sales records or ads, to show your mark's been used in commerce or gained recognition.
  - **Amend your application**: Fix errors, like updating your goods/services description or disclaiming a descriptive word (e.g., "Bakery" in SMITH'S BAKERY).
  - **How to file**: Responses go through the USPTO's online system (TEAS). Keep it professional—think of it as a business letter, not a casual email.

Pro tip: Even if an issue seems small (like a typo in your class description), give it a full, thoughtful response. Half-measures can lead to delays or a flat-out rejection.

When It Gets Complicated

Some Office Actions are straightforward—like swapping out a blurry specimen. Others, especially substantive refusals, can feel like a legal maze. Here's where things get tricky:

- **Complex refusals**: Take "likelihood of confusion." You'd need to analyze how similar the marks really are, how related the goods/services are, and how they're marketed—all while citing past USPTO decisions or legal standards. "Descriptiveness" might mean proving "secondary meaning" (that customers link your mark to your brand), which takes evidence like years of sales data.
- **Strategic responses**: You've got options, but they need finesse:
  - **Negotiate**: Call the examiner to clarify or propose a fix (e.g., narrowing your goods to avoid overlap).
  - **Amend:** Tweak your application—like limiting your services to "online retail" instead of "all retail."
  - **Argue**: Use trademark law or prior cases to push back (e.g., "These marks coexist elsewhere, so mine should too").
- **Risks of DIY**: If you're not a lawyer, it's easy to mess this up. A bad argument might lock you into a weaker position, or an amendment might shrink your trademark's scope more than necessary, leaving gaps competitors can exploit.

Pro tip: If the Office Action feels over your head, don't gamble. Complex refusals often need a pro's touch to maximize your chances and protect your brand.

Why Experienced Trademark Counsel Matters

You might be thinking, "I'm a scrappy entrepreneur—I can handle this myself!" For simple fixes, that might be true. But when an Office Action gets complicated, **experienced trademark counsel** can be your secret weapon. Here's why.

Handling Complexity

Trademark law isn't intuitive. It's full of rules, precedents, and jargon that can trip up even the savviest business owner. Counsel brings:

- **Legal expertise**: They know the Lanham Act (the big U.S. trademark law), USPTO guidelines, and court cases inside out. They can spot flaws in the examiner's logic or pull legal levers you'd never find on your own.
- **Stronger arguments**: An attorney doesn't just respond—they strategize. For a "likelihood of confusion" refusal, they might dig into the cited mark's weaknesses (e.g., it's barely used) or argue your customers aren't the same. For "descriptiveness," they'll build a case for secondary meaning with hard data.
- **Example:** Imagine your mark BLUEWAVE gets refused for confusion with BLUETIDE. An attorney could argue the terms evoke different vibes (waves are dynamic, tides are

predictable) and back it with market evidence —something you might not think to do.

Strategic Advantages

Beyond winning the battle, counsel helps you win the war by strengthening your trademark long-term:

- **Disclaim terms**: Drop a generic word (e.g., "Coffee" in BLUE WAVE COFFEE) to save the unique part.
- **Prove distinctiveness**: Show your descriptive mark's earned a reputation through years of use.
- **Secure consent**: Get the other mark's owner to agree there's no confusion (a formal "consent agreement").
- **Avoiding mistakes**: A DIY response might accidentally limit your rights—like agreeing to a narrow goods description that leaves out future products. Counsel keeps your trademark broad and enforceable.

Example: If you're a craft brewery with HOPHAVEN, an attorney might negotiate a coexistence deal with HOPHILL, instead of fighting a losing battle, saving you time and keeping your brand intact.

Time and Cost Savings

Hiring a lawyer isn't free, but neither is losing your trademark. Counsel delivers:

- **Efficiency**: They know the system—filing responses fast and right the first time, avoiding back-and-forth with the USPTO.
- **Long-term value**: A solid response means a stronger trademark, reducing risks of future disputes or rebranding costs (which can run thousands for a small business).

  Pro tip: If your Office Action is more than a quick fix, invest in counsel. The upfront cost beats the headache of a refused application or a weak mark that can't protect your brand.

Conclusion

An Office Action isn't the end of your trademark journey—it's a fork in the road. How you handle it shapes whether your brand gets the protection it deserves. Let's recap:

- **Deadlines**: You've got **three months** to respond, no exceptions (unless you want to pay $125). Mark it, plan it, do it—abandonment isn't an option.
- **Issues**: They could be **substantive** (confusion, descriptiveness) or **procedural** (specimens, classes). Know what you're facing and hit every point.

- **Counsel**: For complex refusals, **experienced trademark counsel** is your ace in the hole—bringing expertise, strategy, and peace of mind.

Final takeaway: Responding to an Office Action is a make-or-break moment for your trademark. Take it seriously, act fast, and don't hesitate to call in a pro when the stakes are high. Your brand's worth it—and with the right moves, you'll come out stronger on the other side.

* * *

Chapter 9
Understanding Trademark Oppositions

Imagine this: You've spent months—maybe years—crafting the perfect name or logo for your startup. You file a trademark application with the United States Patent and Trademark Office (USPTO), and after a nail-biting wait, you get the green light. Victory, right? Not quite. Before your trademark is officially registered, it faces one last test: a **30-day publication period**. During this window, anyone can challenge your application by filing what's called a **trademark opposition**.

So, **what is a trademark opposition**? It's a formal legal challenge lodged by a third party—known as the "opposer"—who believes your trademark could harm their existing rights. This challenge happens after the USPTO approves your application but before your mark is officially registered. The opposer files their case with the Trademark Trial and Appeal Board

(TTAB), a specialized body within the USPTO, aiming to stop your mark from crossing the finish line.

Why is this a big deal? For entrepreneurs like you, a trademark isn't just a legal formality—it's the backbone of your brand. It protects your business name, logo, or slogan, helping you stand out in the market and build customer trust. An opposition can throw a wrench into that plan. It might delay your registration by months or even years, drain your bank account with legal fees, or force you to abandon your mark entirely and start over with a new brand identity. In short, it's a high-stakes hurdle that can disrupt your momentum and threaten everything you've built.

But here's the good news: You don't have to face it blind. In this chapter, we'll unpack **two common types of oppositions** you're likely to encounter as a small business owner: those from **trademark bullies** and those seeking **coexistence agreements**. We'll explore what they are, how they work, and—most importantly—how you can navigate them with practical, no-nonsense strategies. Whether you're staring down a corporate giant or negotiating a peaceful compromise, this chapter will give you the tools to protect your brand without losing your mind (or your budget).

The Opposition Process at a Glance

Before we dive into the specifics, let's get a clear picture of how trademark oppositions unfold. Knowing the process can help you prepare and respond effectively if you're ever in the crosshairs.

Timing: Once the USPTO approves your trademark application, it doesn't go straight to registration. Instead, it's **published in the Official Gazette**, a public record maintained by the USPTO. This kicks off a **30-day window** where anyone who thinks your mark infringes on their rights can file an opposition. Think of it like a public comment period—except instead of opinions, you might get a legal fight.

How it works: If someone files an opposition, the case moves to the **Trademark Trial and Appeal Board (TTAB)**. The TTAB acts like a mini-court within the USPTO, handling disputes over trademark registration. Both you (the applicant) and the opposer present evidence and arguments—think witness statements, sales data, or examples of customer confusion. The TTAB then decides whether your mark can be registered or if the opposer's challenge holds water.

Possible outcomes:

- **You win**: The TTAB dismisses the opposition, and your mark gets registered as planned. Hallelujah!
- **They win**: The TTAB sides with the opposer, and your mark is blocked from registration. Back to the drawing board.

- **Everyone wins - Settlement**: Here's the twist—many cases never make it to a final ruling. Instead, the parties negotiate a deal, like tweaking your mark or signing a coexistence agreement (more on that later), and the opposition gets dropped.

The process isn't quick. A simple case might wrap up in a few months, but if it goes to a full hearing, you could be looking at years. For a busy entrepreneur, that's time and energy you'd rather spend growing your business. That's why understanding your options —and acting fast—is key.

Type 1: Oppositions by Trademark Bullies

Who Are Trademark Bullies?

First up, meet the heavyweights of the opposition world: **trademark bullies**. These are typically **large corporations** with deep pockets, aggressive legal teams, and a take-no-prisoners attitude. They file oppositions not just to protect their trademarks but to throw their weight around, often targeting startups and small businesses like yours. Why? Because they know you might not have the resources—or the stomach—to fight back.

Their **goal** isn't always about proving your mark will confuse customers or hurt their brand. Often, it's about intimidation. They want to pressure you into abandoning your mark and rebranding, even if your trademark or the goods and services you offer aren't identical to theirs. It's less about legal merit and more about flexing their muscle to keep the competition in check.

Example: Picture a small coffee shop in Austin called BREW HAVEN. A global coffee chain with a similar-sounding name—like BREW HEAVEN—files an opposition, claiming potential customer confusion. The marks aren't exact, and the local shop's artisanal vibe is miles apart from the chain's mass-market model, but the chain doesn't care. They're betting the little guy will cave rather than face a legal brawl.

The Costs and Timeline

Facing a trademark bully is like stepping into the ring with a heavyweight champ. Here's what you're up against:

- **Financial hit**: Defending an opposition can get pricey—fast. Legal fees can easily climb into the **tens of thousands of dollars**, and if the case drags on, you might hit six figures. For a startup scraping by on tight margins, that's a gut punch. You're paying for attorneys, filing fees, and possibly expert witnesses, all while keeping your business afloat.
- **Time drain**: A full-blown opposition can stretch over **years**. The TTAB process involves discovery (gathering evidence),

motions, and potentially a hearing—each step eating into your schedule. That's time you're not spending on product launches, marketing, or customer growth. Meanwhile, your trademark hangs in limbo, leaving your brand in a vulnerable spot.

- **Rebranding option**: Here's the alternative: You could abandon your mark and file a new trademark application for a different name or logo. The filing fee is just a **few hundred dollars**—a fraction of the cost of fighting. Sure, it stings to ditch a brand you've built, but sometimes it's the smarter financial move.

Pro tip: Do the math early. Weigh the cost of defending your mark against the cost of rebranding, and don't forget the hidden costs— like lost time and stress.

Strategic Considerations

When a trademark bully comes knocking, you've got a tough call to make. Here are the factors to weigh:

- **Cost vs. fight**: Is your mark worth the battle? If you've invested heavily in your brand—think logos on packaging, a loyal customer base, or a killer domain name— fighting might make sense. But if you're still early-stage and haven't sunk much into it, rebranding could be less painful than you think.

- **Negotiation potential**: Bullies aren't always out for blood. Some might back off if you offer concessions, like tweaking your logo, changing your tagline, or limiting your goods/services to avoid overlap. It's not ideal, but it could save you a fortune in legal fees.
- **Brand impact**: Rebranding isn't just about money—it's about your customers. Will they follow you to a new name? What about your social media handles, website SEO, or printed materials? On the flip side, fighting a bully could rally your audience around your underdog story—assuming you can afford the fight.

Example: Take that BREW HAVEN coffee shop. The global chain demands they abandon the name. The shop's owner crunches the numbers: $30,000 to defend the mark versus $2,000 to rebrand as HAVEN BREWS (with a new logo and a fresh trademark filing). They negotiate with the chain, offering to tweak the logo and limit their menu to local-roasted beans. The chain agrees, and the opposition is withdrawn—crisis averted.

Key takeaway: Trademark bullies are daunting, but you're not powerless. Assess your resources, explore negotiation, and pick the path that keeps your business moving forward.

Type 2: Oppositions for Coexistence Agreements

What Are Coexistence Agreements?

Not every opposition is a David-and-Goliath showdown. Sometimes, the opposer isn't trying to crush you—they just want to share the sandbox. That's where **coexistence agreements** come in. These are **contracts** between you (the applicant) and the opposer that allow both trademarks to coexist by setting clear rules to avoid confusion in the marketplace.

These oppositions are often filed by **companies with valuable brands** who want to protect their turf without fully blocking your mark. They're less about intimidation and more about drawing boundaries so both businesses can operate without stepping on each other's toes.

Example: A startup called PEAK PULSE, which makes fitness trackers, gets opposed by PEAK PULSE PERFORMANCE, a company selling energy drinks. Instead of demanding a full stop, the drink company suggests a coexistence agreement: the startup sticks to wearable tech, while the opposer keeps the name for beverages. Both brands survive, no courtroom required.

How They Play Out

Coexistence agreements are usually **easier and faster to settle** than bully battles. They typically settle along these lines:

- **Market sectors**: You might agree to limit your mark to specific industries or products— like tech gadgets versus food and drink in the PEAK PULSE example.
- **Visual branding**: You might commit to distinct logos, colors, or fonts to differentiate your look (e.g., bold red for them, cool blue for you).
- **Marketing channels**: Agreeing to sell through different avenues—like online-only for you and retail stores for them—can reduce overlap.

Resolution: These cases often end with a handshake (or at least a signed document) after straightforward negotiations. Both sides want a practical solution, not a drawn-out war. The TTAB might never even get involved if you settle early.

> **Pro tip**: Don't rush to sign. Make sure the terms leave room for your business to grow and thrive.

Strategic Considerations

Negotiating a coexistence agreement is less about

survival and more about strategy. Here's what to focus on:

- **Term scrutiny**: Dig into the details. Does the agreement restrict you from expanding into new markets or product lines? If PEAK PULSE agrees to only make fitness trackers, what happens if they want to launch a workout app later? Push for flexibility where it counts.
- **Future fit**: Think long-term. Where do you see your business in five years? If the agreement locks you into a narrow niche, it could stifle your growth. Negotiate terms that align with your vision.
- **Balance**: Aim for fairness. The opposer wants to protect their brand, but you deserve room to build yours. Don't be afraid to counter-propose adjustments—like tweaking limits or adding a clause for future review.

Example: A bakery called SWEETBLOOM gets opposed by SWEETBLOOM FLORALS, a flower shop chain. They agree the bakery can use the name for baked goods, while the florist keeps it for plants. The bakery's lawyer negotiates an online sales exception, ensuring they can ship cookies without breaching the deal.

Key takeaway: Coexistence agreements can be a win-win, letting you keep your mark with some guardrails. Just make sure the deal supports your business today and tomorrow.

Practical Tips for Facing an Opposition

Whether you're up against a bully or hashing out a coexistence deal, these tips will help you tackle an opposition like a seasoned pro:

- **Move fast**: You've got **40 days** from the opposition notice to file a response with the TTAB. Miss that deadline, and you could lose by default. Mark your calendar, set alerts, and don't procrastinate.
- **Get a lawyer**: The TTAB isn't DIY territory. A **trademark attorney** can navigate the legal maze, negotiate settlements, or argue your case if it goes to a hearing. Yes, it's an expense—but it's cheaper than losing your mark.
- **Keep records**: Document everything—every email, phone call, and draft agreement tied to the opposition. If negotiations sour or the case escalates, a solid paper trail can save your bacon.
- **Think business**: Look beyond the legal fight. How much is your mark worth to your brand? What's the cost—financial and emotional—of rebranding? Could a settlement preserve your momentum better than a win? Crunch the numbers and weigh the stakes.

- **Stay flexible**: Most oppositions—up to 70% by some estimates—end in settlements, not TTAB rulings. Be open to compromise, whether it's tweaking your mark or signing a coexistence deal. Rigidity can cost you more than it's worth.

Key advice: Don't go it alone. Oppositions are complex, and the stakes are high. A good attorney can turn a potential disaster into a manageable bump in the road.

Conclusion

Trademark oppositions can feel like a storm cloud over your entrepreneurial dreams, but they're not the end of the road. Here's the rundown:

The two types in a nutshell:

- **Trademark bullies**: These are the wealthy giants swinging their legal fists to intimidate you into rebranding. Defending against them can mean **expensive battles** or a tough call to pivot, but with the right strategy, you can stand your ground or cut your losses smartly.
- **Coexistence oppositions**: These come from brand-focused companies looking for a workable deal. They're **less costly and quicker to resolve**, often ending in

agreements that let both marks live with clear boundaries.

Big lessons:

- **Be ready**: Before you file a trademark, know the risks. A thorough pre-filing search can flag potential opposers, giving you a heads-up to tweak your mark or brace for a fight.
- **Lean on experts**: Don't skimp on legal help. A trademark attorney can spot pitfalls, negotiate deals, and keep your brand safe— worth every penny for peace of mind.
- **It's doable**: Oppositions aren't a death sentence. With smart planning and a cool head, you can come out the other side with your business intact.

Closing note: Getting an opposition notice can feel overwhelming, like a legal monster lurking in your inbox. But it's just a hurdle, not a wall. With the right approach and support, you can clear it and keep building the brand you've poured your heart into.

* * *

Chapter 10

Keeping Your Registrations in Good Standing

You've crossed a major milestone—your trademark is registered, and your brand has a legal shield. But here's the reality check: a trademark isn't a one-and-done deal. It's a living asset that demands ongoing attention to stay protected and enforceable. Think of it like a car—skip the oil changes, and it'll break down when you need it most. Neglect your trademark, and you risk losing your registration, weakening your rights, or leaving your brand vulnerable to competitors and copycats.

For busy entrepreneurs, trademark maintenance might sound like just another task on an endless to-do list. Between launching products, managing cash flow, and keeping customers happy, legal upkeep can feel like a low priority. But it doesn't have to be complicated or time-consuming. It boils down to three core habits: **using your brand consistently**, **filing renewals on time**, and **stopping infringers**

before they gain traction. Get these right, and your trademark will remain a powerful tool to protect your business for years to come.

In this chapter, we'll walk through each of these areas with straightforward advice and real-world tips. Whether you're a startup founder juggling a million things or a small business owner wearing every hat, you'll find strategies here to keep your trademark in good standing without losing your sanity. Let's dive in.

Consistency, Consistency, Consistency!

Why Consistency Matters

As an entrepreneur, experimentation is in your DNA. You tweak your logo, test new taglines, or add words like "Pro" or "Plus" to see what sticks with your audience. It's how you grow. But when it comes to your trademark, that creative freedom can trip you up if you're not careful.

Here's why: the U.S. Patent and Trademark Office (USPTO) requires proof of use when you renew your registration—examples called "specimens" (think product labels or website screenshots). These specimens must **exactly match** the trademark you registered. If you've changed the wording, redesigned the logo, or even switched the font, your specimen won't align with your registration. The USPTO could reject your renewal, leaving your trademark unprotected. Even worse, inconsistent use over time can erode your legal rights, making it tougher to stop copycats who argue your mark isn't distinctive anymore.

For small businesses, this isn't a minor hiccup—it's a potential disaster. Imagine pouring years into building your brand, only to lose your registration because your logo evolved without proper planning. Consistency isn't just about looking polished; it's about safeguarding the investment you've made in your identity.

How to Maintain Consistency

The fix is straightforward but takes discipline: **use your trademark exactly as it's registered**. Here's how to make it happen:

- **Stick to the original**: If you registered PEAKPULSE as your wordmark, don't start using PEAKPULSE FITNESS on your products or website. That extra word could cause a mismatch at renewal time.
- **Preserve the design**: If your registration covers a black-and-white logo, don't switch to a multicolored version without protecting the new design separately. The USPTO sees these as different marks.
- **File for variations**: Brands evolve—it's natural. If you update your logo or add a tagline, file a new trademark application for

the new version ASAP. This keeps every iteration legally covered.

Pro tip: Create a simple "brand style guide" for your team. It doesn't need to be a glossy 50-page manual—just a one-pager listing your exact trademarked name, logo, colors, and fonts. Share it with everyone who touches your brand: your designer, marketer, even the intern running your Instagram. When everyone's on the same page, consistency becomes second nature.

Examples of Consistency Pitfalls

Let's look at two scenarios small businesses often stumble into:

- **Example 1**: You register FRESHBAKES for your bakery. A year later, you start branding everything as FRESHBAKES HOMEMADE to emphasize your artisanal vibe. At renewal, you submit a specimen showing FRESHBAKES HOMEMADE, but your registration is for FRESHBAKES alone. The USPTO rejects it, and your registration lapses.
- **Example 2**: You register a minimalist black-and-white logo for your clothing line. Over time, you add a splash of red to make it pop. When renewal rolls around, your colorful specimens don't match the original black-

and-white registration, putting your rights at risk.

Key takeaway: Small tweaks can lead to big headaches. Use your mark as registered, and if you pivot, file a new application to lock in the updated version.

Mandatory Renewals

Why Renewals Are Essential

Your trademark registration isn't a lifetime guarantee —it's a renewable lease on your brand's legal protection. Miss a renewal deadline, and your registration can be canceled, stripping away your federal rights. For a small business, that's like handing competitors a free pass to swoop in and confuse your customers—or worse, steal your identity outright.

The upside? Renewals are predictable and manageable if you stay organized. The USPTO sets two main deadlines: one between the 5th and 6th year after registration, and another every 10 years. Hit these marks, and your trademark can last as long as your business does. Let's break it down.

Key Renewal Deadlines

Here are the dates you can't afford to miss:

5th/6th-Year Renewal (Section 8 Declaration):

- **What it is**: Between the 5th and 6th year after your registration date, you must file a Section 8 Declaration proving you're still using your trademark in commerce. You'll need to submit a specimen—like a photo of your product or a webpage screenshot— showing the mark in action.
- **Why it matters**: Skip this, and your registration is canceled. No grace period, no second chances. It's the USPTO's way of weeding out "dead" trademarks that aren't actually in use.

-10-Year Renewal (Section 9 Renewal):

- **What it is**: Every 10 years from your registration date, you file a Section 9 Renewal to keep your trademark active. At the 10-year mark, you'll also file another Section 8 Declaration, so it's a two-for-one filing.
- **Why it matters**: This keeps your registration alive indefinitely, as long as you're still using the mark. Miss it, and you're back to square one.

  Pro tip: Don't rely on the USPTO to remind you —they won't. Set calendar alerts for these deadlines at least six months in advance. Better yet, if you've got a trademark attorney, ask them to track it for you. A little planning now beats a canceled registration later.

Declaration of Incontestability

Want to level up your trademark's strength? Consider filing a **Declaration of Incontestability**:

- **What it is**: After 5 years of continuous use, you can file this declaration to make your trademark "incontestable." It's an optional step, but it's a game-changer.
- **Why file it**: Incontestability narrows the grounds others can use to challenge your mark. They can't claim it's too generic or argue they used it first in some random region. It's not invincible (fraud or abandonment can still undo it), but it's a serious upgrade to your legal armor.

   Pro tip: File this alongside your 5th/6th-year Section 8 Declaration.

Key takeaway: Renewals are your lifeline to keeping your trademark alive. Add incontestability, and you're not just maintaining—you're fortifying.

Stop Infringers Early

Why Early Action Matters

Registering your trademark doesn't mean the USPTO will patrol the marketplace for you. Enforcement is your responsibility, and timing is everything. Let an infringer slide, and you risk diluting your brand, confusing your customers, and facing a legal mess that could drain your bank account. Act fast, and you can often resolve issues cheaply and quietly.

For small businesses, this is critical. You don't have the resources to slug it out in court against a deep-pocketed rival. Delay can escalate a minor annoyance into a full-blown Trademark Trial and Appeal Board (TTAB) fight—think tens of thousands in legal fees and years of stress. Catch it early, and you can use simpler tools to protect your brand without breaking the bank.

- **Monitoring Your Trademark**
- To stop infringers, you first have to spot them. Here's how to keep watch:
- **DIY approach**: Carve out time to search for copycats yourself. Check:
- **Google**: Look for similar brand names or logos in ads and websites.
- **Social media**: Scan Instagram, TikTok, and Facebook for lookalikes.
- **Marketplaces**: Browse Amazon, Etsy, and eBay for knockoffs.
- **Domains**: See if someone's snagged a website mimicking your brand.
- **Professional help**: If you've got the budget, hire a trademark monitoring service. These tools scour USPTO filings for conflicting

applications and can even flag unregistered uses online.

- **Practical tip**: Set up free Google Alerts for your trademark. Type in your brand name, and you'll get an email anytime it pops up online—perfect for catching unauthorized uses fast,

Key advice: Make monitoring routine. Spend 15 minutes a month searching—it's low effort, high reward. Think of it like locking your doors at night: basic security pays off.

Early Enforcement Tools

When you spot an infringer, don't wait—act. Here are two cost-effective ways to shut them down:

Cease-and-Desist Letters:

- **What it is**: A formal letter (ideally from your attorney) telling the infringer to stop using your mark or face consequences.
- **Why it works**: It's fast and cheap—often under $500—and many small-time copycats will comply rather than tangle with a lawyer. It's a warning shot that often ends the fight before it starts.

  Pro tip: Keep the tone firm but professional. You're showing strength, not starting a war.

Letters of Protest:

- **What it is**: A filing with the USPTO to object to a pending trademark application that's too similar to yours. It's free or low-cost ($150 without an attorney's help).
- **Why it works**: If the USPTO agrees, they'll reject the application before it's registered, stopping the infringer in their tracks.

  Pro tip: Timing is key—file before the application is published for opposition (usually within a few months of its filing date).

Example: Imagine you run PEAKPULSE, a fitness app, and spot PEAKPULSE GYM applying for a trademark. You file a Letter of Protest with the USPTO, pointing out the overlap. They deny the application, and your brand stays clear—all without a courtroom.

Key takeaway: Early action beats escalation. Monitor diligently, and use these tools to squash problems before they spiral.

Conclusion

Your trademark is a cornerstone of your business, but it won't protect itself. Keeping it in good standing takes effort— fortunately, it's effort you can handle with a bit of foresight and consistency. Here's the rundown:

- **Consistency**: Use your trademark exactly as registered, and file new applications for any updates. A quick style guide keeps your team aligned.
- **Renewals**: Mark your calendar for the 5th/6th-year and 10-year deadlines. File your Section 8 and Section 9 renewals on time, and toss in a Declaration of Incontestability for extra muscle.
- **Early enforcement**: Watch the market like a hawk, and when infringers pop up, hit them with cease-and-desist letters or Letters of Protest. Quick moves save you from costly battles.

Final takeaway: Trademark maintenance isn't a luxury—it's a necessity. By staying consistent, renewing on schedule, and tackling infringers early, you'll keep your brand secure and your rights rock-solid. It's like routine upkeep for your business's most valuable asset: your identity. With these habits locked in, you can get back to what matters most—building your empire.

* * *

Chapter 11

Beware of Trademark Scams

Imagine you've just submitted your trademark application to the United States Patent and Trademark Office (USPTO). You're excited—your brand is finally on its way to being protected. Then, a few days later, you get an email or a phone call. It looks official, maybe even has the USPTO logo, and it's demanding payment for an "urgent" trademark service. The message warns that if you don't act fast, you'll lose your rights. Something feels off, but you're busy running your startup, and you don't have time to dig deeper. This is exactly what trademark scammers are counting on.

Purpose: Trademark scams are a growing problem, and they're designed to exploit business owners like you. They misuse publicly available trademark data, impersonate the USPTO, and pressure you into quick decisions—usually involving money or sensitive information. These traps can drain your bank account, compromise your personal data, or even cost you control of your brand. This chapter is here to arm you with the knowledge to recognize these scams and avoid them before they do real damage.

Overview: We're going to break this down into three key areas. First, we'll explore the most common types of trademark scams and what they look like. Then, we'll explain why falling for them can hurt your business in ways you might not expect. Finally, we'll give you simple, practical steps to protect yourself. Whether you're new to trademarks or already managing a registered mark, this guide will help you stay one step ahead of the fraudsters.

Common Trademark Scams

Trademark scammers have a playbook, and they use it to target busy entrepreneurs who might not know the ins and outs of the trademark process. Here are the most common scams you're likely to encounter, along with what to watch for so you can spot them in time.

Spoofing Websites and Phone Numbers

Description: Scammers create websites that look almost identical to the USPTO's official site (uspto.gov) or spoof phone numbers to make it seem like they're calling from a government office. These fake sites might use domains like uspto-renewals.com or trademark-office.org, and their goal is to trick you into paying for services you don't need or handing over personal information.

Watch For:

- Website domains that don't end in .gov. The USPTO only uses .gov—anything else (like .com, .org, or .net) is a red flag.
- Phone calls or emails demanding immediate payment for trademark-related services, often with a sense of urgency.
- Requests for sensitive details like your credit card number or Social Security number, which the real USPTO never asks for over the phone or email.

Example: You get an email from info@uspto-services.com claiming you owe $600 to process your trademark application. The site looks polished, but the domain isn't uspto.gov. It's a scam.

Email from Imposters

Description: Fraudsters send emails pretending to be USPTO examiners or officials. They often include details about your trademark—like your application number or brand name—pulled from public records to make it seem legitimate. These emails might ask for payment, request personal data, or threaten to cancel your application if you don't respond quickly.

Watch For:

- Emails that don't come from an @uspto.gov address. Scammers might use something close, like @uspto-notifications.com.
- Demands for fees or information that don't match what's in your official USPTO records (more on how to check those later).
- Typos, odd phrasing, or poor grammar—common slip-ups in scam emails.

Example: An email from examiner.smith@uspto-registrations.org says your trademark will be abandoned unless you pay $400 within 48 hours. The real USPTO doesn't send emails like this from non-.gov addresses.

Fraudulent Solicitations

Description: Companies posing as official agencies send professional-looking letters, invoices, or brochures demanding payment for unnecessary or fake services. These might include "publishing" your trademark in a private directory, "monitoring" your mark for infringements, or "renewing" your registration years before it's due.

Watch For:

- Names that sound official but aren't the USPTO—like "U.S. Trademark Compliance Office" or "Trademark Renewal Agency." The real entity is just "USPTO."

- Urgent warnings that you'll lose your trademark rights if you don't pay immediately.
- Offers for services you didn't request or that sound suspiciously vague or overpriced.

Example: You receive a mailed invoice from "Trademark Protection Services" charging $1,200 to "secure" your trademark. The real USPTO fee for a basic renewal is $325, and they don't send unsolicited invoices.

Why These Scams Matter

Trademark scams aren't just a nuisance—they can hit your business where it hurts. Here's what's at risk and why you need to take them seriously:

Risks:

- **Money Loss**: You could shell out hundreds or thousands of dollars for fake fees or overpriced services that do nothing for your trademark. For a startup scraping by, that's money you can't afford to lose.
- **Data Theft**: Handing over personal or payment information to scammers can lead to identity theft, unauthorized charges, or worse. Your financial security could be on the line.
- **Trademark Loss**: If a scammer hijacks your trademark—say, by changing your USPTO email—they could register it in their name,

sell knockoffs, or demand a ransom to give it back. Your brand could slip out of your hands entirely.

Impact: Let's paint a picture: A scammer takes over your trademark and starts selling cheap, counterfeit versions of your product online. Customers buy them, get disappointed, and leave bad reviews—blaming *you*. Your reputation tanks, sales drop, and you're stuck cleaning up a mess you didn't make. That's the kind of damage these scams can do.

The stakes are high, but the good news is you can avoid these pitfalls with a little know-how. Let's move on to how.

How to Avoid Trademark Scams

Protecting yourself from trademark scams doesn't require a law degree or endless hours of research. It comes down to three straightforward habits: verifying sources, questioning urgency, and staying proactive. Here's how to put them into practice.

Verify Sources

- **USPTO Check**: The real USPTO only uses email addresses ending in @uspto.gov and websites ending in .gov. If you get a message from @trademark-office.com or a similar domain, it's not legit.

- **Use TSDR**: The USPTO's Trademark Status & Document Retrieval (TSDR) system is your go-to tool. It shows all official updates, filings, and communications about your trademark. If a fee or request isn't listed there, it's not real.
- **Protect Passwords**: Never share your USPTO.gov account password with anyone. The USPTO won't ask for it via email or phone—anyone who does is a scammer.

Pro Tip: Bookmark uspto.gov and the TSDR page on your browser. When you get a suspicious message, don't click any links—just go straight to TSDR to check the facts.

Question Urgency

- **No Rush**: The USPTO doesn't call or email you out of the blue demanding instant payment or action. If someone says you'll lose your trademark unless you pay *right now,* they're lying.
- **Call TAC**: When in doubt, call the USPTO's Trademark Assistance Center (TAC) at 1-800-786-9199. They can confirm whether a request is genuine.

Pro Tip: Scammers love to push your panic button. Take a deep breath, double-check the details, and don't let urgency trick you into acting rashly.

Conclusion

Trademark scams are a real threat, but they don't have to derail your business. Scammers thrive on urgency, deception, and your unfamiliarity with the trademark process. Watch for red flags like non-USPTO domains, unexpected payment demands, or pressure to act fast.

Takeaway: You can protect your trademark with vigilance—verify everything through official USPTO channels, question anything that feels off, and don't hesitate to ask for help if you're unsure.

* * *

Chapter 12
Using and Choosing Trademark Counsel

This chapter is your go-to guide for understanding the value of trademark counsel, deciding when to bring one on board, selecting the right attorney for your needs, and working with them to protect your brand. Whether you're registering a trademark, facing a legal dispute, or planning to expand your business, this chapter provides actionable advice to ensure your trademark process goes smoothly.

Starting a business is exciting, but it's also full of risks. Your brand—your name, logo, or slogan—is often what sets you apart from the competition. Protecting it isn't just a legal checkbox; it's a smart business move. That's where trademark counsel comes in. Let's break it down so you can make informed decisions without drowning in legal jargon.

Why Trademark Counsel Matters

A **trademark attorney** is a legal expert who specializes in protecting your brand through trademarks. They're not just someone who fills out forms—they're a partner who helps you avoid headaches and build a strong foundation for your business. Here's why they're worth your time and money:

- **Navigate the Law**: Trademark law isn't exactly user-friendly. The U.S. Patent and Trademark Office (USPTO) has strict rules, deadlines, and requirements that can trip up even the savviest entrepreneur. An attorney knows the ins and outs, ensuring your application doesn't get rejected over a technicality—like picking a mark that's too similar to someone else's or filing in the wrong category.
- **Save Time**: You've got a business to run— chasing customers, managing inventory, or tweaking your website. Do you really have hours to spend researching trademark classes or deciphering USPTO guidelines? Counsel takes that off your plate, handling the paperwork, searches, and legal back-and-forth so you can stay focused on growth.
- **Protect Your Brand**: Your brand isn't just a name—it's your reputation, your identity, and often one of your most valuable assets. A

trademark attorney doesn't just file your application; they help you choose a strong, enforceable mark and defend it against competitors or copycats. They can spot risks (like a rival business with a similar name) before they become problems.

Imagine you've spent months building a killer brand—say, BREWBUDDY for your craft beer startup—only to find out someone else has a similar trademark. Without counsel, you might lose the name, waste marketing dollars, and have to start over. An attorney helps you avoid that nightmare by getting it right from the start.

Hiring counsel isn't about spending money unnecessarily—it's about investing in peace of mind and protecting what you're building.

When to Hire Trademark Counsel

You don't need an attorney for every single trademark task, but some situations scream for professional help. Here's when you should pick up the phone:

- **Complex Applications**: If your trademark is more than a simple word with a simple product—the application process gets tricky. Same goes if you're protecting it across multiple product types (say, T-shirts *and* coffee mugs). An attorney can nail the details and make sure the USPTO doesn't kick it back.

- **Legal Challenges**: If the USPTO sends you an Office Action (a fancy way of saying "we've got a problem with your application") or another business files an opposition to block your trademark, you're in legal territory. These aren't simple fixes—an attorney knows how to argue your case, whether it's proving your mark is unique or negotiating with the other side.

- **International Expansion**: Taking your brand overseas? Each country has its own trademark laws, deadlines, and quirks. Maybe you're eyeing Canada or the EU—great! But you'll need someone who understands international treaties (like the Madrid Protocol) to keep your mark safe across borders.

- **High Stakes**: If your trademark is the heart of your business—like your company name or the logo on every product—losing it could be devastating. Think about a bakery called SWEETRISE—if that name gets challenged and you lose, you're rebranding everything: signs, packaging, ads. The cost of counsel is peanuts compared to that mess.

Now, what about the small stuff? If you're registering a basic wordmark (like MEATDOGZ for dog snacks) and the stakes are low, you might try filing it yourself or using an online service. The USPTO's website has a decent filing system, and it'll cost you less upfront—around $350 per class of goods. But here's the catch: DIY comes with risks. Miss a deadline, pick the wrong class, or skip a proper search, and your application could be dead in the water. Worse, you might infringe on someone else's mark and not even know it until they sue.

So, weigh your options. If your brand is your baby—or if the process feels overwhelming—counsel is the safer bet.

How to Choose the Right Trademark Attorney

Finding the right lawyer is like hiring a key employee—you want someone skilled, trustworthy, and easy to work with. Here's how to pick a winner:

Qualifications to Seek

- **Experience**: You wouldn't hire a rookie to run your marketing team, so don't settle for an attorney who's new to trademarks. Look for someone who's filed hundreds (or thousands) of applications and tackled disputes—like oppositions or infringement cases. They'll know what works and what doesn't.
- **Specialization**: Trademark law is its own beast. An attorney who focuses on it full-time will be sharper than a general lawyer who

juggles divorce cases and real estate on the side. Ask: "Is trademark law your main gig?" If not, keep shopping.

- **Reputation**: Word of mouth matters. Check online reviews or ask fellow entrepreneurs for recommendations. A good attorney should have a trail of happy clients and solid results —like getting tricky marks approved or winning disputes.

Questions to Ask

Before you sign anything, have a chat. Most attorneys offer a free initial call—use it to feel them out. Try these:

- *How many trademark cases have you handled?* (Look for specifics—10 cases? 100?)
- *What's your approach to USPTO refusals or oppositions?* (Do they fight hard or roll over?)
- *How do you charge—hourly or flat fees—and what's the estimated cost for my case?* (Get a ballpark so you're not blindsided.)
- *Can you share examples of similar work you've done?* (Real stories beat vague promises.)
- *How do you keep clients updated?* (Will you hear crickets or get regular emails?)

These questions cut through the fluff and show if they're a fit for your vibe.

Warning Signs

Not every attorney is a gem. Steer clear if you spot these:

- **Guarantees of Success**: "Your trademark's a slam dunk!" Nope. The USPTO is unpredictable—no one can promise approval. If they do, they're either clueless or overselling.
- **Vague Answers About Fees or Timelines**: "Oh, it'll cost what it costs." Uh-uh. You deserve a clear estimate—like $1,500 for a basic filing or $3,000 if it gets messy. Same goes for timelines—6-12 months is normal, but they should say so upfront.
- **Poor Communication or Pushiness**: If they dodge your questions, interrupt you, or pressure you to hire them on the spot, run. You want a partner, not a used-car salesman.

Take your time. Interview a few options, trust your gut, and pick someone who gets your business and your budget. Your brand's too important for a rushed choice.

Working with Trademark Counsel

Hired an attorney? Awesome—now let's make it a smooth ride. Collaboration is everything. Here's how to get the most out of it:

Be Clear: Your attorney isn't a mind reader. Tell them your story: What's your business about? How do you use your trademark (on products, ads, your website)? Any plans to grow—like new products or markets? The more they know, the better they can tailor their work. For example, if you're launching "FitFuel" for protein bars but might add workout gear later, say so—it could shape your application.

Stay Involved: They'll handle the heavy lifting, but don't check out completely. Here's what to expect them to do:

- Run a **trademark search** to check for conflicts (e.g., is "FitFuel" already taken?).
- Draft and file your application with the USPTO.
- Respond to any Office Actions or legal pushback.
- Keep you posted on progress—like when it's filed or if the USPTO needs more info.

If something's confusing—like a weird USPTO notice —ask. It's your brand; you've got every right to understand what's happening.

Manage Costs: Legal fees can add up, but you can keep them under control:

- Agree on a fee structure upfront. Flat fees (e.g., $1,200 for filing) are predictable; hourly rates (e.g., $300/hour) can climb fast if issues arise.
- Prioritize your trademarks. If cash is tight, protect your company name first, then add logos later.
- Ask for estimates for best- and worst-case scenarios—like $1,500 if it's smooth, $4,000 if there's a fight.

Heads-up: the trademark process isn't quick. A typical application takes 6-12 months to get approved—if there are no hiccups. Disputes or backlogs can stretch it longer. Be patient, but don't hesitate to nudge your attorney for updates if you're antsy.

Think of it like a team effort: they're the coach, you're the quarterback. Stay engaged, and you'll cross the finish line with a stronger brand.

Final Thoughts

Trademark counsel isn't just a line item on your budget —they're your partner in locking down your brand and dodging legal traps. By picking the right attorney and working with them like a pro, you'll save yourself time, money, and the stress of fixing mistakes later. It's not about throwing cash at a problem; it's about building a shield around what makes your business special.

Your brand is your story—how customers know you, trust you, and choose you over the next guy. Don't leave it unprotected. With the right counsel in your corner, you'll have the confidence to grow, compete, and thrive. So, take the leap, find your trademark ally, and let's get that brand locked down tight.

* * *

Chapter 13

U.S. Trademarks and The Rest of the World

In today's world, your business doesn't stop at the U.S. border—neither do your opportunities or your risks. Whether you're a startup selling software to clients in Asia, a small business shipping artisanal goods to Europe, or an entrepreneur with dreams of going global, your trademark is your brand's identity. But here's the reality: protecting that identity doesn't happen automatically across borders. International trade is booming, and with it comes the need to safeguard your trademark in every country where you operate—or might one day operate. A competitor in Brazil or a copycat in China could use your brand name if you don't act, and that's a headache no busy entrepreneur needs.

Purpose of This Chapter

This chapter is your roadmap to protecting your

trademark in a global marketplace. We'll break it down into three key areas:

- **For U.S.-based businesses**: You'll learn how the Madrid System can simplify and speed up trademark protection in over 120 countries with just one application—perfect for startups looking to scale internationally without drowning in paperwork.
- **For non-U.S. businesses**: We'll explain the rules for securing a U.S. trademark, including the must-know requirement to hire a U.S.-licensed attorney, so you can confidently enter the American market.

By the end, you'll have the tools to think globally about your trademark strategy—whether you're expanding abroad or bringing your brand to the U.S.

The Madrid System: Fast-Track Protection for U.S.-Domiciled Businesses

Overview of the Madrid System

What It Is:

The **Madrid System** is like a VIP pass for trademark protection. It's a treaty-based system that lets you file one international trademark application through your home country's trademark office—in your case, the U.S. Patent and Trademark Office (USPTO)—and seek protection in multiple countries at once. No need to hire lawyers in every country or wrestle with foreign forms. It's a streamlined solution for busy entrepreneurs who want their brand protected worldwide without the chaos.

Administered by:

The system is run by the **World Intellectual Property Organization (WIPO)**, a United Nations agency based in Geneva, Switzerland. WIPO keeps the Madrid System humming, processing applications and coordinating with member countries.

Scope:

The Madrid System covers **over 120 member countries**, including heavy hitters like the European Union (as a single designation), China, Japan, India, and Australia. Whether you're eyeing one market or dozens, this system has you covered in most of the world's biggest economies.

How It Works for U.S. Businesses

Eligibility

To use the Madrid System, you need a starting point in the U.S.—a trademark application or registration with the USPTO, known as your **basic mark**. This could be a mark you've already registered or one you've filed and plan to take global. Without a U.S. basic mark, you can't access the system.

Process

Here's how it works, step by step:

- 1. **File an international application**: You submit your application through the USPTO, not directly to WIPO. This form lists your basic mark and the countries where you want protection (called "designated countries").
- 2. **Designate desired member countries**: Pick as many of the 120+ member countries as you want. You can start small (say, Canada and the UK) or go big (China, Japan, and the EU).
- 3. **Submit fees**: Costs depend on the number of countries and trademark classes (categories of goods or services) you choose. You pay in U.S. dollars through the USPTO, and they convert it to Swiss francs for WIPO.
- 4. **USPTO forwards to WIPO**: The USPTO checks your application and sends it to WIPO, who reviews it for completeness and distributes it to your designated countries.
- 5. **Local examination**: Each country's trademark office reviews your application under its own laws. If approved, your mark is protected there as if you'd filed locally.

Speed Advantage

Filing separately in each country is a slog—different forms, languages, deadlines, and legal systems. The Madrid System cuts through that mess. One application, filed in English, gets you in front of trademark offices worldwide faster than you could say "international expansion."

Example: Imagine you run GROWEASY, a U.S.-based gardening tool company, and you're launching in Germany and South Korea. Without Madrid, you'd file separate applications in each country, hire local attorneys, and wait months. With Madrid, you file once through the USPTO, and within 12-18 months, both countries could grant your protection.

Benefits for U.S. Businesses

Efficiency

Why file five applications when one will do? The Madrid System lets you handle everything through the USPTO in English—no translating documents or chasing foreign deadlines. It's a time-saver for entrepreneurs juggling a million tasks.

Cost Savings

Filing individually can cost $500-$1,000 per country, plus legal and translation fees. Madrid's fees are often lower (starting around $100-$300 per country, depending on the market), and you pay once upfront. For a small business, that's real money back in your pocket.

Flexibility

Your business isn't static, and neither is the Madrid System. If you expand to new markets later, you can add countries to your international registration without starting over. It grows with you.

> **Pro Tip**: Use the WIPO's online fee calculator to estimate costs before you file—it's a quick way to budget your international strategy.

Key Considerations

Dependency

There's a catch: for the first **five years**, your international registration depends on your U.S. basic mark. If your U.S. mark gets canceled—say, because someone challenges it or you miss a deadline—your international protections can collapse too. It's critical to keep your U.S. trademark solid.

Local Review

The Madrid System simplifies filing, but it doesn't guarantee approval. Each country examines your application under its own rules. A mark that's fine in the U.S. might get refused elsewhere if it's too similar to an existing trademark or doesn't meet local standards.

Example: GROWEASY might breeze through in the U.S. and EU but hit a snag in Japan if a similar mark, GROW EZ, is already registered for tools. You'd need to address that refusal with Japan's trademark office, possibly hiring local counsel.

Key Takeaway: The Madrid System is a powerful tool, but it's not foolproof. Protect your U.S. mark and be ready for a few bumps abroad.

Foreign Counsel Rules for Businesses Domiciled Outside the U.S.

USPTO Requirement for U.S.-Licensed Attorneys

Mandate

If your business is based outside the U.S., here's a non-negotiable rule: you **must hire a U.S.-licensed attorney** to file a trademark application or handle any proceedings with the USPTO. This applies to startups in London, small businesses in Sydney, and everyone in between.

Purpose

The USPTO isn't trying to make your life harder. This rule ensures foreign applicants follow U.S. trademark law, which can be tricky, and keeps the system fair and fraud-free. A U.S. attorney acts as your guide, making sure your application meets all the requirements.

No Exceptions

There's no workaround. You can't file directly, use a non-lawyer, or rely on your local attorney back home.

Without U.S. counsel, your application won't even get off the ground.

Practical Implications

Finding Counsel

Hiring a U.S. attorney sounds daunting, but it's manageable:

- **Referrals**: Ask business contacts who've worked in the U.S. for recommendations.
- **Legal Directories**: Sites like Martindale-Hubbell or Avvo list qualified trademark attorneys.
- **Google**: Search for an online law firm that specializes in U.S. trademark law.

Role of the Attorney

Your U.S. counsel isn't just a formality—they're your partner. They'll:

- File your trademark application and handle all USPTO correspondence.
- Advise on U.S.-specific rules, like proving "use in commerce."
- Respond to office actions (USPTO requests for clarification or fixes).
- Represent you in disputes, like if someone opposes your mark.

Cost

Fees depend on your case. A simple application might run $500-$2,000, while complex issues (like fighting a refusal) cost more. For access to the U.S. market—worth billions—it's a worthwhile investment.

Example: You're a Brazilian coffee roaster, "Café Rio," wanting a U.S. trademark. You hire a U.S. attorney who files your application, ensures your packaging meets U.S. standards, and gets your mark registered in under a year.

Key Takeaway: Think of U.S. counsel as your ticket to the American market. They're not a hurdle—they're your bridge.

Foreign Ownership of U.S. Trademark Registrations

No Limitations on Foreign Ownership

Equal Opportunity

Good news: there are **no restrictions** on foreign businesses owning U.S. trademarks. Whether you're in Tokyo or Toronto, you can register and own a U.S. trademark just like a U.S.-based company. The process might require a U.S. attorney, but once your mark is registered, your rights are the same.

Requirements

You'll need to follow standard U.S. trademark rules:

- Show your mark is used in U.S. commerce (or file based on intent to use, followed by proof later).
- File maintenance documents (e.g., renewals every 10 years) to keep your registration active.
- Use a U.S.-licensed attorney for all USPTO dealings.

Counsel Requirement

Even after registration, foreign owners must use U.S. counsel for filings or disputes. It's a consistent rule, but it doesn't limit your ownership rights.

Why It Matters

Market Advantage

A U.S. trademark isn't just legal protection—it's a business asset:

- **Credibility**: It tells customers and partners your brand is legit and protected in a major market.
- **Enforcement**: If someone copies your mark in the U.S., your registration lets you sue in federal court or block infringing imports.

Accessibility

The U.S. doesn't care where you're from—you don't need a U.S. office or citizenship. This openness encourages foreign businesses to invest in U.S. trademark protection without extra hoops.

Example: A Korean skincare brand, GLOW SEOUL, registers its mark in the U.S. before selling on Amazon. When a knockoff appears, they use their registration to shut it down fast, protecting their reputation.

Key Takeaway: The U.S. trademark system is a global equalizer. If you're eyeing the American market, securing your mark is wide open to you.

Conclusion

Summary

Your trademark is your brand's passport—don't let it get stuck at the border. Here's what we've covered:

- **U.S. Businesses**: The Madrid System is your fast track to protecting your mark in over 120 countries. One application through the USPTO can save you time, money, and stress as you grow globally.
- **Non-U.S. Businesses**: U.S. trademarks are yours for the taking, but you'll need a U.S.-licensed attorney to make it happen. Once registered, foreign owners enjoy the same

rights as U.S. companies—no restrictions, just opportunities.

Next Steps

Going global isn't a solo mission. Whether you're a U.S. startup eyeing Europe or a foreign business targeting the U.S., talk to a trademark attorney. They'll help you weigh your goals—do you need Madrid now? Is a U.S. mark your priority?—and guide you through the process. Your brand deserves protection wherever your customers are.

* * *

Chapter 14
Free Trademark Resources

This chapter provides a curated list of free, reliable resources to help you understand and manage the trademark process. Whether you're researching, applying for, or maintaining a trademark, these tools and guides are essential for businesses seeking high-level information without the need for costly services.

Free U.S. Trademark Searches (performed by attorneys)

Website: https://www.markavo.com

Key Features:

- Receive a no-obligation, free trademark search performed by a trademark attorney within one business day. Look for the "free trademark search" button at the top of the website.

- Get U.S. attorney representation when filing this trademark application for industry leading flat-rate fees, if you so choose.

Official Government Resources

Government websites are the most authoritative sources for trademark information. They offer step-by-step guides, legal requirements, and tools to help you through the application and registration process.

U.S. Patent and Trademark Office (USPTO)

Website: www.uspto.gov/trademarks

Key Features:

- Trademarks Basics: https://www.uspto.gov/trademarks/basics. A beginner-friendly guide to understanding trademarks.
- Trademark Electronic Application System (TEAS): https://www.uspto.gov/trademarks/apply/teas. Free online filing system with help sections.
- Trademark Status & Document Retrieval (TSDR): https://tsdr.uspto.gov. Track your application status and retrieve documents.
- Trademark Electronic Search System (TESS): https://tess2.uspto.gov. Search existing trademarks to avoid conflicts.

Trademark Manual of Examining Procedure (TMEP)

The TMEP is a detailed resource for understanding how the USPTO evaluates trademark applications, available for free online.

Website: Trademark Manual of Examining Procedure: https://www.uspto.gov/trademark/laws-regulations/trademark-manual-examining-procedure-tmep

Key Features:

- Official USPTO manual outlining the procedures for examining trademark applications.
- Includes sections on application basics and legal standards.

Legal Associations and Educational Resources

These organizations provide free educational materials, articles, and webinars to help you understand trademark law and best practices.

International Trademark Association (INTA)

INTA offers expert insights and educational content, helping you stay informed on trademark trends and legal developments.

Website: https://www.inta.org

Key Features:

- Publications, webinars, and articles on trademark registration and protection.
- Global perspective on trademark issues, useful for businesses considering international expansion.

American Bar Association (ABA) - Intellectual Property Law Section

Articles, FAQs, and guides on trademark law written for both legal professionals and business owners.

Website:https://www.americanbar.org/groups/intellectual_property_law.html

Key Features:

Articles, FAQs, and guides on trademark law written for both legal professionals and business owners.

Cornell Law School - Legal Information Institute (LII)

Website: https://www.law.cornell.edu

Cornell LII offers a legal foundation for understanding trademark statutes and case law, ideal for businesses seeking a deeper understanding.

Key Features:

- Free access to the U.S. Code on trademarks (15 U.S.C. § 1051 *et seq.*).
- Case law summaries and explanatory articles on trademark law.

World Intellectual Property Organization (WIPO)

Website:https://www.wipo.int

WIPO provides a broader context for businesses considering international trademark protection.

Key Features:

- Resources on the Madrid System for international trademark registration.
- Guides and articles on global trademark practices

Conclusion

These free resources provide a solid foundation for understanding the U.S. trademark application and registration process. By leveraging official government tools, educational materials from legal associations, and practical online services, you can navigate the trademark system confidently and cost-effectively. Always verify information through official sources like the USPTO to ensure accuracy and compliance.

About Markavo.com

Markavo® is a leading provider of trademark protection services, dedicated to offering businesses of all sizes a **simple, fast, and economical approach** to safeguarding their intellectual property. Since **2021**, we have been committed to helping businesses protect their trademarks in the **U.S. and worldwide**, ensuring their brands are secure and their investments are safeguarded.

With a focus on **cost-effectiveness** and **efficiency**, Markavo® has earned the trust of **over 6,000 businesses**. Our experienced team of attorneys and trademark specialists is passionate about providing top-notch service and support, ensuring that our clients' trademark needs are met with professionalism and expertise.

Can You Trademark It? Find Out.

At Markavo®, we understand the importance of knowing whether your desired trademark is available. That's why we offer a **free trademark search service**, conducted by an attorney, with results delivered within **one business day**. This allows you to make informed decisions about your trademark strategy and avoid potential conflicts.

Flat Fee Rates for Trademark Registration

We believe in transparent and affordable pricing. Our **flat fee rates** for registering a new trademark start at just **$99 in legal fees**, making it easier than ever for businesses to protect their brands without breaking the bank.

Save $50 on Your First Order

To help you get started on your trademark protection journey, we're offering a special discount of **$50 on your first order**. Simply use the coupon code **MARKAVOBOOK** at checkout to take advantage of this limited-time offer.

At Markavo®, we're more than just a trademark service provider – we're your partner in brand protection. Let us help you secure your business's future with our comprehensive trademark solutions.

·

www.ingramcontent.com/pod-product-compliance
Lightning Source LLC
Chambersburg PA
CBHW050508210326
41521CB00011B/2373